ROCKHOUNDING
Washington

A Guide to the State's Best Sites

LARS W. JOHNSON

FALCONGUIDES

GUILFORD, CONNECTICUT

FALCONGUIDES®

An imprint of The Rowman & Littlefield Publishing Group, Inc.
4501 Forbes Blvd., Ste 200
Lanham, MD 20706
www.rowman.com

Falcon, FalconGuides, and Make Adventure Your Story are registered trademarks of The Rowman & Littlefield Publishing Group, Inc.

Distributed by NATIONAL BOOK NETWORK

Copyright © 2018 The Rowman & Littlefield Publishing Group, Inc.

Maps © The Rowman & Littlefield Publishing Group, inc.
All photos by Lars W. Johnson unless otherwise noted

British Library Cataloguing-in-Publication Information available
Library of Congress Cataloging-in-Publication Data available

ISBN 978-1-4930-1909-0 (paperback)
ISBN 978-1-4930-1910-6 (e-book)

♾™ The paper used in this publication meets the minimum requirements of American National Standard for Information Sciences—Permanence of Paper for Printed Library Materials, ANSI/NISO Z39.48-1992.

Printed in the United States of America

CONTENTS

Overview

ACKNOWLEDGMENTS

This part is still and always will be like winning a shiny golden award on TV and getting to give my shout outs. Even though I won't be shuffled off stage by music, I still hope I don't forget anyone who helped to make this dream happen.

My family has always been the biggest supporters of my dreams and aspirations. I always start by thanking them first: my mother, Kristi Robinson; my stepfather, Denis Harnish; my papa, Jerard Johnson; my stepmother, Karen Johnson; "Grandma Beach," Lorraine VanBrocklin; my little brother, Karl Johnson; and my stepdaughter, Sophia, for being entertaining and patient while her mother and I hunt rocks for hours on end. I could not have done any of this without any of you. Thank you all for always having a place to rest my dirty head and a warm meal, even at the last minute.

I really want to thank my friends who accompanied me in the field when I didn't want to do a recon trip alone; people such as my "little sister," Kelley Harmon; Ian Jackson; Kyle Heflebower; Nadia Ricci; Michael Casper; and especially Avery "Skunk Dawg" Steen, who went on more failed trips with me than anyone. I want to thank Chris Sheckla for supplying me with the camera I used for this book; everyone at the *Mount Hood Rock Club*, especially Barbra Brandt, Linda Honeycutt Frenette, Greg Gentry, Alison Jean Cole, Tim Fisher; everyone in the *NW Rockhounds* group especially Lanny and Juliet Kittleson, Jake Rankin, Rodger Kilmer, Arthur Ortiz, and Dawn Fredricks; the whole crew at The Gold Door, thank you all for covering shifts so I could be on the road; Ed Lehman and Bob O'Brien of the WSMC; Logon Appleyard and Dave McFarland for supplying photos; the five dudes who helped me break into my truck at Rock Creek; Toyota, for making the awesome Tacoma that has gotten me to more rockhounding sites in the NW than I can count; Les Schwab Tires, especially the Maple Valley location; and the music of the Melvins and Big Business for keeping me insane and awake while driving night and day, all over Washington, researching this book.

I especially want to thank my wife. Without her I could not have gotten through the trials and tribulations I went through writing this book. She found so many of the best rocks on our adventures and would quite often find the prize just as I was about to give up on a site. She is my rockhounding Viqueen, and I'm awfully fortunate to have her in my life. Thank you, Amber. I love you with all my heart.

This book is dedicated to Grandma Beach.

INTRODUCTION

I thought writing a guidebook about the state I live in was an honor, but now that I've gotten to write a guidebook for my home state; the place I fell in love with rockhounding, I can't even put it in to words. Washington proved to be a tough mistress when it came to giving up her gems and minerals. She locked me out of a lot of places and it was difficult to find accessible sites in the great state I was born in. In no way is this book complete, but again it never would be.

I still believe that rockhounds should share their knowledge of the hobby with each other. Keeping each other informed and updated about old and new sites is a vital element to keep our hobby a rolling stone. Remember, most of these sites are on *public* land and we, the people should all have an opportunity to equally enjoy our great mineral rich lands. We are rockhounds after all, not gold miners <wink>, and we should always be willing to share our experiences and collecting localities with other rockhounds. You don't necessarily have to hold someone's hand and lead them to a pit, but some directions on a map and some suggestive guidance can really encourage the rockhounding spirit. Share what you find and you will be rewarded with the same.

I have personally visited and collected at every site mentioned in this book, with the exception of Timberwolf Mountain and The Rock 'N' Tomahawk Ranch. Sometimes the cards just don't line up. Sometimes a fee ranch closes early for the season. Each site in this book gets my personal seal of approval. If I didn't think it was a collectable site, it didn't make it in this book.

For my Oregon book I listed some road stats, such and miles driven, milkshakes drank, and waypoints taken. This round I didn't keep as much track of that stuff. Washington also does not have as many random paces in the high desert to get milkshakes. I did notice, however, that in northeastern Washington people really seem to like soup to go. We kept seeing it advertised as gas stations and convenient stores. What's up with that northeast Washington? I believe though, that I drove more miles for Washington than I did Oregon. I also blew a lot fewer tires in Washington. I will say Oregon seems to have more milkshakes in the middle of nowhere, perfect for a hot day.

A view of Diablo Lake. One of the many spectacular views seen on the way to rockhounding locations.

This book can be used in a variety of ways. First and foremost, you can use the sites to plan the ultimate Washington rockhounding adventure. Some people, including myself, have used guidebooks like this as a personal site checklist. I write notes all over my books; I add my own GPS coordinates, correct typos of mileage, and any information I may need to remember about a particular site or material. I hope you to do the same with this book and use it as a tool to expand your own reference of Washington. My favorite copies of my books are the ones that are falling apart from use, written all over, and full of sticky notes. It makes me so happy to see people using the information and getting out there.

WASHINGTON ROCKHOUNDING

Washington is host to a wealth of rocks, gems, and minerals. From the hot high desert in the east to the chilly Pacific Ocean in the west, Washington has a lot to offer the northwest rockhound. As I mentioned before, Washington was a harsh mistress. Finding accessible land can be difficult, to say the least. I've noticed that Washington rockhounds, not all, but some, seem to be much more tight-lipped about their digging sites. With limited access, I can understand why. I'm curious which site or sites in this book will upset someone because I gave away their "secret spot." I can understand. Garret Romaine put my "secret spot," Short Beach, in his update to Gem Trails of Oregon. I tried very hard to have different beaches listed in my book versus his, but sug nubbits, Short Beach is MY beach, so I had to put it in *Rockhounding Oregon*. Now I have so many people who are mad at me for giving away their secret spot too. Ah, the life of a guidebook author.

In the process of writing this book, I got to collect a few new minerals that I have never found before. Before this book I had never collected hematite, stilpnomelane, chrysoprase, or blue beryl. I am glad to have some minerals checked of the old list. As much as I love collecting agates, it sure was fun to change things up a bit.

Participating in a rock club can be an excellent way to learn more about the hobby, to work with hard-to-get lapidary equipment, and to meet a lot of other people with rocks in their heads just like you. Joining a rock club can also be a great way to gain access to lands that are not generally open to rockhounds. The Washington State Mineral Council hosts multiple rockhounding trips throughout the year and they quite often get access to collecting sites the general public just can't go.

There are also many rockhounding groups and forums to be found on the internet. I have been a part of many, if not all of them. I was recently asked to be an administrator for the Facebook group, NW Rockhounds. The group is recognized as a club by the Mineralogical Federation, but they don't operate like a normal club. We don't have dues, meetings on odd nights and our number one rule is BE NICE. Our group has an annual campout the weekend after Memorial Day weekend and we have an annual BBQ at the club headquarters in Seattle. Members will often set up small meetups and

The best rock shop in Washington.

digs throughout the year and it is a great way to meet like-minded folks. Through NW Rockhounds I have made friends that I will have for life. I have made business partners who are also in the rock business as I am. For me, the absolute best thing about being a member of NW Rockhounds is the group where I met my wife. We went on a date and never stopped talking rocks since. NW Rockhounds makes good things happen.

OFFICIALLY WASHINGTON

Banded agate from Iron Springs.

- **State Gem—Petrified Wood**

Yes, the official Washington State Gem is a fossil. I'm very surprised it wasn't elected the "state rock" and Ellensburg Blue Agate elected "state gem." The agate everyone is so crazy over got nothing. Even so, Washington is host to several petrified forests. Gingko Petrified Forest is one of the better known ones and even has a museum and nature walk. You cannot collect there, but places where you can are nearby. Petrified wood was designated the state gem in 1975.

- **State Fossil—Columbia Mammoth**

The students of Windsor Elementary School can be thanked for out extinct pachyderm state mascot. They fought for 4 years to finally have it designated "state fossil" in 1998. The mammoth's roamed the North American continent during the Pleistocene age. Fossilized remains of the Columbian mammoths have been found in the Olympic Peninsula. The collecting of vertebrate fossils is prohibited on public land, so you're not likely going to add one to your collection. You can, however, collect metasequoia fossils, the Oregon State fossil, and many Washington fossil localities.

COLLECTING REGULATIONS

- **Minerals**

The Bureau of Land Management, United States Forest Service, and the Department of Natural Resources consider amateur rockhounding an outdoor recreation. Just like fishing and other outdoor activities approved on public lands, rockhounding is not without its rules and regulations. Recreational noncommercial collecting is allowed using hand tools only.

There are a few rockhounding sites located on public lands that are close to Wilderness Study Areas or Wilderness Area. While on BLM land you are allowed to dig holes. When on wilderness land, rockhounding is limited to surface collection only, with digging off limits. In 2012, the BLM put restrictions on beach agate collecting, limiting all beach collecting to a 1-gallon bucket full per day, but not to exceed 3 gallons per year.

- **Petrified Wood**

The collection of petrified wood is allowed on public land. A federal law passed in 1962 states that rockhounds are limited to collecting 25 pounds plus one piece per day, but not to exceed 250 pounds per person per year. People may not pool their limits together to obtain pieces weighing over 250 pounds. The removal of petrified wood weighing over 250 pounds may only be done so with a permit.

- **Fossils**

Common invertebrate and plant fossils (such as snail, clam, and leaf fossils) may be collected on public lands for noncommercial personal use. The collection of any vertebrate fossils or other paleontological resources is prohibited without a permit. Paleontological Resources Preservation under the Omnibus Public Lands Act of 2009 defines a paleontological resource as: any fossilized remains, traces, or imprints of organisms, preserved in or on the earth's crust that are of paleontological interest and provide information about the history of life on earth. A paleontological resource permit is required to collect paleontological resources of scientific interest. Anything collected with a permit will remain the property of the United States and will be preserved for the public for scientific research and education.

NW Rockhound, Logon Appleyard, busting open some rock at Walker Valley. Photo by David McFarland

- **Artifacts**

All historic and prehistoric remains on public land are protected by law. This includes, but is not limited to arrowheads, points, feathers, whole or broken pots, stones tools, basketry or even old bottles. Artifacts were first protected under the Preservation of American Antiquities Act of 1906. The Federal Land Policy and Management Act of 1976 and The Archaeological Resources Protection Act of 1979 later added even more laws protecting these artifacts. The excavation, destruction, vandalism, or removal of archeological resources (historic and prehistoric) from public lands is punishable by law.

TOOLS AND SUPPLIES

The most important tool you will use on every single rockhounding trip is your brain. Be safe, be smart, be aware, and be very prepared. Be safe, and know your physical limits before traversing the terrain. Be aware of your surroundings and any obstacles they may contain, be it crumbling terrain, fast river currents, or any potentially dangerous local flora and fauna, such as poison oak or rattlesnakes. There's an area in Washington nicknamed "Dead Rockhound Gulch." Many people have died there over the years because they were not using common sense. They collected in an unsafe area and paid the ultimate price, just to collect quartz crystals. No rock is ever worth losing your life over. Use good judgment when collecting at any site. Now that the serious part is over, let's get to the fun stuff: tools!

Like my Papa always says, you need the right tool for the job. Being a hardware store owner, he knows a thing or two about the subject. Rockhounding is no exception! Be prepared for the task at hand. To begin, there is a huge difference between a rock hammer and a carpenter's hammer. Rock hammers and geology picks are tempered to withstand repeated heavy blows to hard rock. Carpenter hammers are designed for nails and can easily splinter or break causing great bodily injury when used on rocks. Do not use them for rockhounding at any cost. The best rock hammers and picks are made from a solid piece of steel, versus hammers with the head and neck being composed of different materials. My personal favorite rock hammers are made by Estwing. Rockhounds and masons have trusted this brand's durability and design for decades.

Geology picks are probably the most useful and recognizable tool of the rockhound. With one blunt end and the other pointed, a geology pick can be used to hammer, pick, and pry material out of the ground or host rock. They can come in many lengths and weights. Find which size works best for you. Being 6'4", I like the E3-23LP by Estwing, as the handle is a bit longer than the others. Find a model that works the best for you.

The next tool most used by rockhounds is a sledgehammer. They are used to bust open rock and to pound chisels and gads into cracks in host rock. Sledgehammers start at 3 pounds and work their way up to 16 pounds. Like choosing a geology pick, find the size and weight of sledgehammer that works best for your needs.

A large agate that was trying to hide in the mud at the Washougal River.

For breaking up large pieces of rock, such as basalt, and exposing pockets of minerals within, chisels, gads, star drills, wedges, and pry bars are essential. Chisels are hand tools with a flat end; gads are the same, but with a pointed end; star drills have a star shaped end. All are struck with a hammer or sledge to split the rock open. Miners digging geodes at Walker Valley in Washington have come up with some ingenious wedges used for cleaving large pieces of basalt. Truck springs have been cut and filed into a wedge shape. They call these basalt splitters "Walker Valley Wedges." Pry bars are used to move material or pop it out of the host rock. They can range from a foot and a half to several feet in length. Paint scrapers are used to split and expose layers of shale when hunting for fossils.

If digging is the chosen method of attack at the site, an array of shovels and trowels are necessary. Both spade and flathead shovels are useful depending on the site. Small folding shovel and garden trowels are good excavators when working in tight spaces. I've always had a personal connection with shovels. I love to digs holes and take great pride in doing it well. Jessica Shenk of the Spectrum Sunstone Mine and High Desert Minerals once complimented Kelley Harmon and me on the cleanest and neatest hole she's ever seen dug at the mine. High five! I also once got this compliment from my father and I will not confirm nor deny I cried a little.

Picks are also another essential tool needed when digging a hole. They tear up tough dirt and make shoveling it out a heck of a lot easier. Estwing make a fantastic pick called the Paleo Pick and I love it. That little thing can really tear up some dirt. Common mining picks and awls work great too.

Always wear eye protection when wielding tools. Protect your hands with a well-fitting pair of gloves and consider wearing a handkerchief over your face when dust or flying rock chips are present. Screens are useful for the collection of some material such as sunstones and smaller material at some sites such as Hampton Butte. You can find them in some rock shops, prospecting stores, and online. I prefer to make my own and have a collection of screens in various sizes for various purposes.

Spray bottles, a bucket of water, and an old tooth brush or nail brush are great to have around for washing off stubbornly sticky dirt to better judge material. Wetting down some minerals, especially silicates such as agate and jasper, can also give you an idea of what it will look like when it is polished.

Something to carry and store the treasures you find is very important as well. Fossils need special consideration; initially wrapping them in paper towels or newspaper will protect them on the trip home, as much of the material is rather fragile. Keep a box of freezer bags and a permanent marker with your supplies. The bags are great for storing your smaller finds and to keep material from different sites separated. The sharpie comes in handy for labeling. Sometimes after a long rockhounding trip you can forget what rocks came from which site. A small bucket, backpack or shoulder bag is fine when collecting beach agates and other small float material. When the material starts to get big, the tried and true classic way to carry and store minerals is the plastic 5-gallon bucket. A lot of rockhounds have a huge amount of 5-gallon buckets sitting around filled with material, and I am no exception. I'm constantly on the hunt for more buckets; I never seem to have enough. There is now a golf-style caddie with wheels that holds a 5-gallon bucket. Another good method for carrying heavy rocks is a sturdy metal frame backpack. Tony Funk of *idahorockshop.com* swears by this method and that man moves a lot of rocks.

TOP TEN WASHINGTON ROCKHOUNDING SITES

With a nod to Garret Romaine's *Rockhounding Idaho*, this is my personal top-ten list for Washington. These are places I continue to visit year after year and never seem to tire of collecting at. They are also places a person can go for the first time and find success. In no particular order, I present to you my list:

- Hansen Creek for quartz and amethyst.
- Saddle Mountain for petrified wood.
- Damon Point for beach agates.
- Sol Duc River for orbicular jasper.
- Rock 'N' Tomahawk for Ellensburg Blue Agate.
- Red Top for blue agates and geodes.
- Walker Valley for geodes.
- Salmon Creek for carnelian.
- Fossil Creek for fossils.
- Stubbs Hill for jasper.

HOW TO USE THIS BOOK

Land type: A brief description of the terrain you can expect to be in at the digging site. West of the Cascades is mostly forested. East of the Cascades is mostly high desert sagebrush with some pockets of forest.

County: What county the digging site is in.

GPS: Lists the GPS coordinates of the particular site or sites. I used a plethora of devices to take my readings and then checked them on Google Maps for accuracy. Google Earth can also be a good resource for researching the terrain of a site you intend on visiting.

Best season: The weather can ultimately determine the outcome of any rockhounding trip. One thing for certain in Washington is that it is going to rain. Even in the summer, it rains. While rain and storms make for great beach collecting, it turns eastern Washington roads into a nasty gumbo that even the best 4WD vehicles can get stuck in. Always check weather reports before heading out on any rockhounding trip. No matter what the weatherman predicts be prepared for any type of weather. It's been said that if you don't like the weather in Washington, wait ten minutes. Conditions can change quickly.

Certain times of the year better lend themselves to the type of rock-hounding you will be doing. For instance, late summer is best for river and creek collecting as the water is low, exposing more gravel bars. Knowing when to be in a particular area greatly increases your chances of success finding material.

Land manager: It's very important to know what land you're planning to collect on. Always check with the land manager for the status of each site before you visit. Collecting rules, regulations, and land access are always subject to change. Always contact the land manager before dedicating a long drive to a site that may have changed hands or may be unexpectedly inaccessible due to snow, rain, landslides, wildfires, and so forth. This can change at a moment's notice. Two months after *Rockhounding Oregon* was released things changed and now I'm going to have to yank two or three sites when I update.

Material: This section lists what types of rocks, gems, and minerals you can expect to find when visiting the site. Material is generally listed from most to least abundant. More detailed descriptions will be found in the rock-hounding section of each site.

Tools: This section will help guide you to what tools you will need to bring for success. Sometime many tools are listed for a site, depending on what you're looking to remove. I personally never go out without being armed with a plethora of tools and accessories for those just-in-case moments. When exploring you can run into materials that need a completely different set of tools to collect. I've often found myself in the middle of the high desert, wishing for a tool I left at home in the basement. On that note, I have also made it home realizing I left my favorite pick 400 miles away in the high desert. I now spray-paint some of my tools bright with fluorescent colors, purple is my favorite, to make them noticeable in the dirt, reminding me to pick them up.

Vehicle: Recommends the type of vehicle you will need to gain access to a site. Some places you can bring a minivan packed with the whole family and the dogs, while others you absolutely need high-clearance 4WD to get anywhere near the site. Don't exaggerate your vehicle's capabilities. Be fully practiced in driving your vehicle both forward and backward. Washington has some very remote collecting sites where you don't want to get stuck because you decided to push the limits with your vehicle. Take it from Ol' Uncle Lars, because I have and it got me into some dangerous situations.

Accommodations: Lets you know if camping or lodging is available in the area. Most sites open for collecting are on BLM land, which is generally open for primitive camping and many sites have camping on site. Many sites nearby may have nicely developed camping facilities available and others will be dry or primitive. Several Falcon Guides as well as many publications and online forums are dedicated to Washington camping and can be a great resource for finding that perfect spot to stay.

Special attractions: Listed are mostly sites of geologic, scenic, or historic interest. Take some time to stop at vistas, points of interest, and historical markers. Bringing along guidebooks such as *Hiking Hot Springs in the Pacific Northwest* and *Roadside Geology of Washington* can add other fantastic places to visit and a better knowledge of the state on your travels.

Finding the site: In this section, you will find detailed directions to the digging sites or sites in an area. I used Google Maps for directions and it seems to be pretty accurate. Every vehicle reads mileage just a little bit different, so don't get all bent out of shape over a tenth of a mile or two. I tried to list all mileposts, mines, signs, and other pertinent landmarks to help you find the way. Remember that roads are always subject to change and /or closure. Always check with the land manager for current road status. Signs can sometimes be hidden by vegetation, stolen, damaged, worn, in disrepair, or vandalized to the point you could use the sign itself to screen rocks. I've noticed people seem to love to shoot signs out in the middle of nowhere.

Rockhounding: This section goes into more detail about what you can expect to find at a particular site, how to dig it, and anything else you should know about a site or the area you're in. Though not a focus, any recommendations for nearby gold panning may also be also found in this section. With the exceptions of Rock 'N' Tomahawk Ranch and Timberwolf Mountain I visited every site in this book and more. While researching I found that much information in other guidebooks and websites had changed, even in the 4-5 years of them being published. I tried to keep information as up-to-date as possible. Like any other resource, the information found in this book is subject to change and it likely will. Again, always check with the land manager on the status of any site.

Map Legend

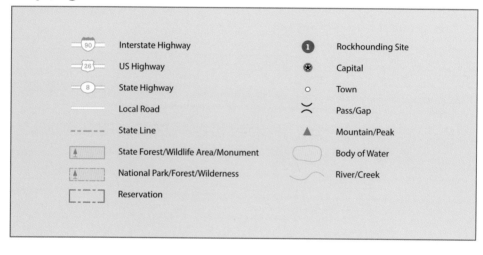

90 Interstate Highway	1 Rockhounding Site
26 US Highway	Capital
8 State Highway	○ Town
Local Road	Pass/Gap
State Line	▲ Mountain/Peak
State Forest/Wildlife Area/Monument	Body of Water
National Park/Forest/Wilderness	River/Creek
Reservation	

ROCKHOUNDING SITES

The beginning of it all.

1 Puget Sound

At Grandma's house strolling the beach where I first discovered rockhounding.
Photo by Amber lee Johnson.

Land Type: Sound shorelines
County: Multiple
GPS: Site A: N48 8.543' / W 122 46.927', 3 ft. (North Beach Park); Site B: N47 21.678'
/ W123 9.351', 3 ft. (Potlach State Park); Site C: N47 39.646' / W122 25.972', 3 ft.
(West Point Lighthouse Beach); Site D: Site E: N47 58.912' / W122 30.849', 4 ft.
(Double Bluff Beach); Site F: N48 25.315' / W122 39.650', 11 ft. (Rosario Beach);
Site G: N48 42.838' / W122 54.377', 7 ft. (North Beach); Site H: N48 46.358' / W122
31.955', 2.5 ft. (Locust Beach)
Best Season: Any
Land Manager: Multiple
Material: Quartzite, quartz, jasper, agate, chalcedony, petrified wood, epidote,
granite, banded gneiss, jade, serpentine, conglomerates, zeolites, fossils, and
sea glass
Tools: Gem scoop

Vehicle: Any
Accommodations: Yes and no. Depends on where you are.
Special attractions: The Puget Sound is the attraction.
Finding the site: Google Maps or Waze is your friend here.

Rockhounding

I really could have stuffed this book full of beach after beach found on the Puget Sound. While that helps plump up the book I really don't like repeating myself and I'm sure you don't want to read the same information over and over again either. In this chapter, I lumped together ten of my favorite places to visit when traveling near the Puget Sound. The sound has 1,332 miles of shoreline. There is a lot of rocky shoreline in all those miles and I'm sure you'll find your favorite place too. Keep in mind that Washington has private beaches. Even though I was born in Washington and my rockhounding roots started on a private Puget Sound beach, having lived in Oregon for so long, private beaches don't make sense to me anymore. They should belong to the people. That being said, respect any private property signs you may encounter.

My wife looking for Orbicular Jasper at Pilchuck State Park.

Sites 1-2

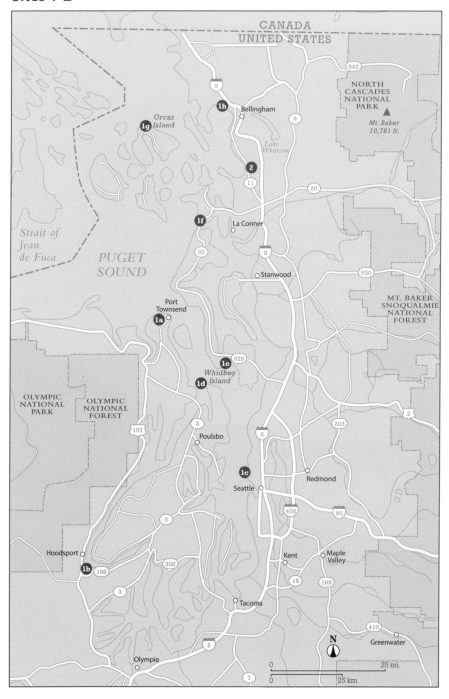

When it comes to gravel on the Puget Sound it can be said that all the beaches are the same, yet all the beaches are unique. What I mean by this is there is a lot of common gravel found in the sound that was ushered in from elsewhere. Rocks from Alaska, Canada, Idaho, and Montana have been found in the gravels. When it comes to locally sourced material some beaches may have more of one thing than another. For example, rocky beaches found near the mouths of jade-producing rivers such as the Skagit will likely have more jade to be found. Potlach State Park is just north of the mouth of the Skokomish River. The Skokomish is known for its red jaspers and that material can be found in abundance at the state park. This all being said, you may find jade and jasper on any beach that was brought in via glaciers and floods from Canada or other places. So much can be collected on the Puget Sound it's almost impossible to list it all.

As I've mentioned many times, I got my start rockhounding on a Puget Sound beach when I was 4 years old at my grandmother's house. I used to call her Grandma Beach because of where she lived. My grandmother, who lived next to cows, was not so fond of the moniker I gave her as a young child. I still look for agates on that very same beach to this day. I think this is why I absolutely feel right at home walking gravels next to bodies of water. At grandma's beach I don't always find anything, but I always find myself. With the many options for beachcombing on the sound, I truly hope you find your beach that you return to year after year.

2 Blanchard Hill

A piece of stilpnomelane found sitting on the ground.

Land Type: Forested Roadcut
County: Skagit
GPS: N48 36.781' / W122 23.666', 282 ft.
Best Season: Spring through fall
Land Manager: Washington State Department of Natural Resources
Material: Stilpnomelane
Tools: Heavy hammers, picks, gads, geology pick
Vehicle: Most
Accommodations: None on site; lodging in Bellingham
Special attractions: Sammish Overlook
Finding the site: From I-5 take exit 240. Take Lake Samish Rd. west for about 0.5 mile. Take a left onto Barrell Springs Rd. and dive 0.7 mile. Take a right onto 5 Mi Blanchard Hilltrail and follow this for 2 miles where you will the dig site on your right. It's very obvious.

Rockhounding

Stilpnomelane is an iron-rich variety of phyllosilicate. The name is derived from the Greek *stilpnos* for shining and *melanos* for black. As this site and true to its name the stilpnomelane is found as shiny radiating black crystals in white to clear quartz. The veins of quartz streak through a massive deposit of chert. This mineral is mostly of specimen interest, but a skilled lapidary can turn out some wonderful cabs from this material as well.

First thing is first. Please only collect a small amount of material at this easily accessible rockhounding site. A small specimen for your collection is just fine, especially if you don't know how to cut it. Let's be sure that this location is taken care of and available to rockhounds for generations to come. Washington is limited in collecting locations as it is and we don't need to lose any more to over digging.

Collecting fine specimens here can be as difficult or as easy as you want it to be. To take the easy route just search for small- to medium-sized pieces found in the talus (loose rocks) of the road cut. You should be able to locate with ease a fine specimen or two for your Washington mineral collection. To

Inspecting the cut for large chunk of workable stilpnomelane.

A cut slab of stilpnomelane. (Lehman collection)

Cabochons of stilpnomelane cut by wagonmaster, Ed Lehman. (Lehman collection)

obtain larger specimens suited for cutting slabs from, it's going to be much more difficult. This is going to involve some hard rock mining. Bring your favorite chisels, gads, and a heavy hammer to free larger chunks from the green chert host. Find yourself a nice chunk and just stick with that one large piece. Again, we want to keep this site around for some time to come.

At the end of your collecting day, be sure to make the short trip up the road to the Samish Overlook at the top of the hill. From there you can experience a breathtaking view of Samish Bay, the San Juan Islands, the Samish River Delta, and on a clear day the Olympic Mountain Range. People often paraglide from this location and that can be a lot of fun to watch. If your day ends at sunset you're in for a real treat up at the overlook. I recommend you bring your favorite person along for some smooching.

3 Murdock Beach

The orbicular jasper tends to be very bright and easy to spot on the shoreline.

Land Type: Ocean beach gravel
County: Clallam
GPS: N48 9.248' / W123 51.640', 6 ft.
Best Season: Any. Discover pass required
Land Manager: Washington State—Department of Natural Resources
Material: Agate, chalcedony, jasper, orbicular jasper, porphyry basalt, calcite pseudomorphs, and much more
Tools: Gem Scoop
Vehicle: Any
Accommodations: Campgrounds in area
Special attractions: Olympic National Park
Finding the site: Take WA-112 just west of Port Angeles. Drive for about 16 miles then take a right onto PA-S-2500. Drive 0.3 mile then turn right onto PA-S-2510. It's about a half mile to the parking area. It's about a 0.25 mile hike to the beach from here.

Sites 3-6

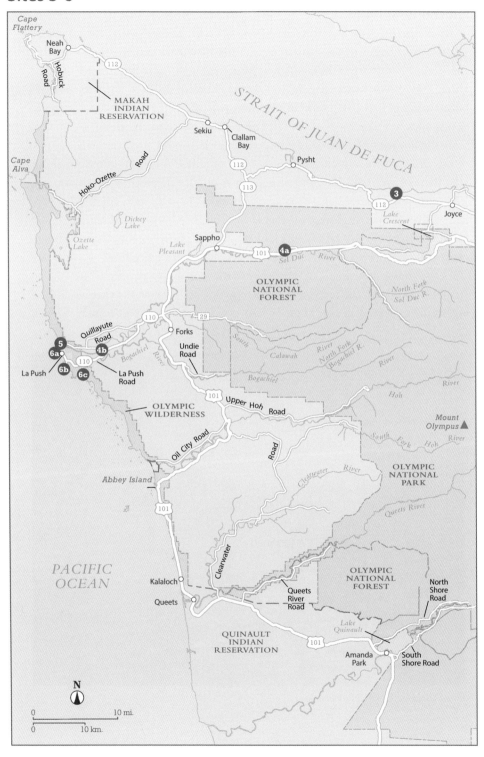

Cape
Flattery

Neah
Bay

Hobuck
Road

112

MAKAH
INDIAN
RESERVATION

Cape
Alva

Hoko-Ozette Road

Sekiu

Clallam
Bay

112

STRAIT OF JUAN DE FUCA

Pysht

113

3

112

Joyce

Lake
Crescent

Dickey
Lake

Ozette
Lake

Lake
Pleasant

Sappho

101

4a

Sol Duc River

North Fork
Sol Duc R.

OLYMPIC
NATIONAL
FOREST

Quillayute

110

Road

29

Forks

South

Calawah

River

North Fork

Bogachiel R.

River

5

6a

110

4b

La Push

6b

6c

La Push
Road

Bogachiel

River

Bogachiel

River

River

101

Upper Hoh

Road

Hoh

OLYMPIC
WILDERNESS

Oil City Road

Road

Mount
Olympus ▲

South Fork

Hoh

River

Abbey Island

Clearwater River

OLYMPIC
NATIONAL
PARK

101

Queets River

PACIFIC
OCEAN

Clearwater

Kalaloch

Queets

Queets
River
Road

OLYMPIC
NATIONAL
FOREST

North
Shore
Road

Lake
Quinault

QUINAULT
INDIAN
RESERVATION

101

Amanda
Park

South
Shore Road

N

0   10 mi.
0   10 km.

Rockhounding

This is one of those beaches that have a little bit of everything for everyone. I can't even begin to imagine where all the heavily ocean worn pebbles that are found here started their journey. Many of these rocks could have worked their way down from Canada and Alaska. The stones here are very smooth from years of being tumbled in the turbulent waters of the Strait of Juan De Fuca. This is a worthy place to have an expert geologist tag along just to sort out the amount of rocks and minerals you can find. I was somewhat happy I was alone on this adventure as only I had to answer my own questions about the identity of rocks. Many of which I had no clue. From this beach you can also clearly see Victoria, Canada across the strait.

During my visit, I was of course keeping my eyes peeled for agate and jasper as they are my favorites. I did find a few good specimens including a very nice piece of orbicular jasper. The agates and chalcedony are in tones of grey and yellow, but I'm sure there's the possibility of other colors. The jasper is mostly in the red tones, but keep your eyes peeled for that wonderful Olympic orbicular jasper. There is also good porphyry basalt which is black

Inspecting material a Murdock Beach.

to grey matrix with radiating white feldspar crystals that can often look very flower like and why this rock is sometimes known as Chrysanthemum Stone. There are reports of calcite pseudomorphs that form in an array of shapes. They are known as glendonites. I didn't find any, but like I said my eyes are trained for agate and jasper. Keep your eye out for just about anything at this beach. I wouldn't be surprised if other cool rocks can be found like jade or petrified wood working their way down from Canada and Alaska.

Down the road is Twin River park and about a quarter mile down the beach from there is a known fossil concretion deposit that often have crab fossils trapped inside. There is also good beach gravel access found here. The problem here is there is now a sign at the park that states you are not allowed to collect rocks. Nearby Harrison Beach Campground has beach access, but you must make reservations ahead of time and be staying at the campground to access the beach.

4 Sol Duc River

A large chunk of orbicular jasper found in the Sol Duc River.

Land Type: Forest river
County: Clallam
GPS: N48 3.944' / W124 7.135', 736 ft.
Best Season: Late spring through fall
Land Manager: USFS—Olympic National Forest
Material: Jaser, orbicular jasper
Tools: Geology pick, gem scoop
Vehicle: Any
Accommodations: Camping on site
Special attractions: Olympic National Park
Finding the site: Take US 101 to about 35 miles west of Port Angeles and about 20 miles east of Forks. Look for the sign to Klahowya Campground. Park in the day-use area and find your way to the river, preferably to a part with gravel.

Rockhounding

This was a site that almost got away from me. I visited it on a solo whirlwind tour of the peninsula and I hit a lot of sites that day. I didn't take enough notes, had the 1st Annual NW Rockhounds BBQ the next day, and, well if you were there you know what happened. Needless to say, I erased a few things out of my mind. Come about a year later when I'm piecing sites together for this book, I come across some pictures of a river I didn't quite recognize and some huge pieces of orbicular jasper. It took me a couple of days and some digging in old texts to realize I stopped at the Sol Duc that day too. I'm sad to say there were two other locations like this that I still am not 100 percent sure about. I think they are the Cispus and Wind Rivers over by Mt. St. Helens, but I apparently didn't take any GPS that day, thinking I would remember. Take it from Ol' Uncle Lars, and take notes. There would be two more sites in this book if I had.

The Klahowya Campground is a lovely place to stay and gives you access to excellent gravel bars. Park in the day-use area and pay the modest fee. If you're cheap and adventurous you might be able to access the river by parking

The Sol Duc River offers the rockhound many gravel bars to explore.

by the bridge and working your way down to the river. Honestly, I think that's what I did. After touring for two books, these sites can start to bleed together. Remember: notes.

Wander the plentiful gravels of the Sol Duc River in hunt of a good chunk of orbicular jasper. I happened to stumble across a very large chunk immediately and found many other small one good for tumbling. The orbicular jasper here can have quite a bit of hematite in it, the hematite mages for wonderful metallic contrast against the red jasper. A word of warning; hematite streaks blood red; that's how it got its name. Cutting anything with significant hematite content in a rock saw will cause the oil to turn a blood-red color. Some people don't mind this, some people do.

There are many other pullouts and parks along the Sol Duc River, so bring a map and do some exploring. A word of warning I hear there are glittery hipster vampires in the town of Forks and they will bore you to death. If you can avoid them, then Forks is a lovely town to stay in. Well, there was that one time in a motel that I saw a bedbug and ended up sleeping on top of a wooden table. I'm not going to name the place because they were super nice, quickly fixed up a room that was not ready, and gave me a discount after I mentioned the bug problem.

5 Rialto Beach

Small smooth orbicular jasper found in the gravels of Rialto Beach.

Land Type: Ocean beach
County: Clallam
GPS: N47 55.239' / W124 38.356', 9 ft.
Best Season: Fall through winter
Land Manager: USNPS—Olympic National Park
Material: Orbicular Jasper, Quartzite, Chalcedony, Agate, Petrified Wood
Tools: Collecting bag
Vehicle: Any
Accommodations: Camping at site and in area
Special attractions: Olympic National Park
Finding the site: From US-101 take WA-110 W for 7.8 miles to Mora Rd. Turn right onto Mora and drive just a little over 5 miles to the parking area. From here head to the beach and the gravel.

Rockhounding

Rialto Beach is not far north from First Beach but takes a long drive around Quillayute River to reach. While this site is a national park, where collecting is usually prohibited, light beachcombing is permitted, which is considered about a handful. If you are caught with buckets and you're trying to fill them up, you may get a talking to or more from a park ranger. Stick to just taking a few souvenirs home from this beautiful and picturesque beach.

The material most sought at Rialto Beach is high quality orbicular jasper. Most pieces you will find are not going to be much bigger than an inch, but you might get lucky with a few larger pieces. The jasper at this beach had been tumbled around for quite some time. While small they tend to be very hard and great for tumbling. You might even be able to skip the first stage of grit as they are already well-rounded. You will also find lots of white quartzite, plain red jasper, and a few agates and chalcedony. The orbicular jasper is the star of the show here.

The shoreline gravel goes on for what seems like forever. One could spend nearly all day wandering the miles of rocks. I did a little walking until

Collecting on less than favorable days gives you the beach almost all to yourself.

I found a nice flattish area. I was there at the wrong time and the tide was coming in. It still didn't stop me chasing and running from waves as they churned up the gravel exposing new material with each retreat. That is also one of my favorite sounds in the world; the tumbling of rocks in an ocean wave. After a while, I noticed people were watching me. I tend to make a lot of noise and talk, maybe yell, at the ocean. At first, I felt a bit silly, but then they started to do the same thing. They weren't as quick and got hit by a wave. Take it from Ol' Uncle Lars and don't do this. Chasing waves can be very dangerous and you could get overwhelmed by a wave and even worse get hit by hard to see floating driftwood. I just have a pension for danger and I've been doing it my whole life. Now and then the ocean gets me and it always reminds me of her awesome power.

6 The Number Beaches

A couple of orbicular jaspers found at First Beach.

Land Type: Ocean shoreline
County: Clallam
GPS: Site A: N47 52.663' / W124 35.207', 0 ft. (Third Beach); Site B: N47 53.113'
/ W124 37.245', 0 ft. (Second Beach); Site C: N47 54.439' / W124 38.354', 0 ft.
(First Beach)
Best Season: Winter
Land Manager: A: Quileute Reservation; B & C: BLM—Olympic National Park
Material: Agate, chalcedony, jasper, orbicular jasper
Tools: Gem scoop, geology pick
Vehicle: Any
Accommodations: Camping allowed with permit on Second and Third Beaches.
Lodging in nearby towns.
Special attractions: Sparkle vampires in Forks
Finding the site: Weather traveling north or south on US-101 find your way to
WA-110 north of Forks. Take WA-110 for 12 miles. At this point, you will see parking

for Third Beach Trailhead. Second Beach Trailhead parking is another 1.1 miles west. First Beach is another 1.2 miles into La Push. Turn right onto Alder, then left onto River St., then another left on an unnamed road to the parking area.

Rockhounding

I call these the "number beaches," well, because that's what they are. Long time ago a creative literary genius went ahead and named these three consecutive beaches First Beach, Second Beach, and Third Beach. Were you able to pick up on my sarcasm there? It can sometimes be tricky to appreciate in writing.

The beaches just so happen to rank themselves in progressive difficulty to reach. First Beach you can drive right up to. Second Beach requires a 1.4 mile round-trip hike. Third Beach is a 2.8 mile round-trip hike. The good news is the more difficult the hike, the less populated the beach will be, and therefore the gravel will be much less picked over. My friend and lapidary, Keith Allen (@k.allen_lapidary), reports that he has found some of the biggest beach agates he's ever collected at Second Beach.

Even in the summer when there's not a lot of gravel, orbicular jasper can still be found.

Many people have questioned the status of collecting at all three of these beaches. First Beach is on the Quileute Reservation, but a handful of beach rocks as souvenirs are acceptable. Second and Third Beach are a part of the Olympic National Park. Usually the collection of anything in national parks is strictly prohibited. In this case, they allow some light beachcombing and consider a handful a good amount. Be sure to call and check in with the National Parks Service in case this policy changes. I would hate to see anyone get in trouble just for picking up a handful of beach rocks.

You will find similar material at all three sites. Be on the lookout for agate, chalcedony, jasper, orbicular jasper, petrified wood, and possibly jade. First Beach has more orbicular jasper than agate. It is reported to me from rock-hound friends that there is generally more agate at Second and Third Beaches. This can all change with a good storm. Being easy to access First Beach is very populated, but even with a packed summer beach I still managed to find a handful of excellent orbicular jasper.

7 Skokomish River

A cut slab from a piece of swirly jasper found in the Skokomish River. Photo by AMBER LEE JOHNSON.

Land Type: Forest river
County: Mason
GPS: Site A: N47 24.522' / W123 18.523', 514 ft. (SE of campground); Site B: N47 25.055' / W123 19.736', 570 ft. (near bridge).
Best Season: Late spring through fall
Land Manager: USFS—Olympic National Forest
Material: Red jasper, orbicular jasper, agate, chalcedony
Tools: Geology pick (for prying)
Vehicle: Any
Accommodations: Camping at Brown Creek Campground; anywhere on BLM land
Special attractions: Potlach State Park
Finding the site: From I-5 in Olympia take US-101 exit and travel for about 27.6 miles. At this point take a left onto W Skokomish Valley Rd. and drive 5.6 miles to Covey Rd. Follow Covey to the right (it will turn into NF-23) and continue another

9.6 miles. Take the NF-2348 to the right and drive about 0.6 mile until you cross the Skokomish River over a bridge. Once you reach this point you have two options. You can take the road to the right, pay for a campsite, and find access through the campground. Southeast of the campground is some really good gravel that I marked as Site A. Check Google Earth to get an idea of where they are. The other option is to continue on the road to the left and continue for about 0.2 mile. Here you will see a bridge. You can park before the bridge or after you cross. I guess it all depends on available parking and how you feel at the moment. After you decide where to park find your way down to the river and start heading upstream. There are some huge gravel beds down that way. Just keep walking.

Rockhounding

If brick-red to slightly bright-red jasper is your jam, then the Skokomish River is the spot for you. The material is absolutely everywhere. Most of it is very hard and will take an excellent polish. Some will be brecciated and have spots filled in with quartz or agate. There is also a bunch of porous wannabe red stuff around, but the jasper is not hard to distinguish. Now that I've said

There are plenty of gravel bars to explore at Skokomish River.

that, what we were looking for here was a beautiful Olympic orbicular jasper. The material can be undeniably stunning when you find a good piece and it can make for some awesome lapidary material, but it is nowhere as abundant as the plain red jasper littered all over this river. Make sure to get any suspect dry material wet in the river so help bring out the orbs. Keep an eye out for agates and chalcedony as well.

Just as with any river hounding adventure you will want to bring some sort of rubber boots, waders, or your best river shoes. You will be crossing the river a lot and you will get a bit wet. We explored this area in early October just before the rain really started kicking in. The river was very low and easy to navigate with only a couple deep spots to cross. The river will be much higher in spring and you should absolutely expect to get very wet if you should decide to cross anywhere. Also, be careful while walking through the forested edge of the river as my wife was attacked and stung by hornets taking a shortcut along the riverbank. It may have just been her dumb luck, but I feel I should report on it.

A large chunk of jasper found in the Skokomish River. It showed signs of possible orbs, so we carried this one out.

Sites 7-11

There is excellent camping available in the immediate area. Brown Creek Campground has twenty camping sites to choose from and a few of them are right on the river. There are also camping spots near the bridge and parking area. The best site, in my humble opinion, can be found just a few hundred yards upstream once you get to the Skokomish River from the bridge parking area. You will have to pack in everything and cross the river a few times to get to this wonderful spot, but if you're up for it I highly recommend it. There is a nice fire pit made of stacked river stones and some large stones right next to it for relaxing on. Nothing like sitting on rocks, in front of a roaring fire, while inspecting the treasures you found during the day.

8 Iron Springs

The biggest and best from Iron Springs. Don't get excited. It's not always like this.

Land Type: Creek and ocean gravels
County: Grays Harbor
GPS: N47 9.526' / W124 11.395', 10 ft.
Best Season: Winter
Land Manager: BLM—Spokane
Material: Agate, chalcedony, carnelian, jasper, orbicular jasper, jade, and petrified wood
Tools: Gem scoop
Vehicle: Any
Accommodations: Camping and lodging up and down the coast
Special attractions: The Ocean is the attraction.
Finding the site: There are many ways to reach this site, but with all of them you will need to end up on WA-109. Coming from north or south on WA-109 make your way to the Iron Springs Resort north of Copalis Beach and south of Ocean Grove. Do not park at the resort. Please park just off the road at the east end of the inlet. The trail is at the south end.

Rockhounding

This is a great and not so great kind of site. Like any ocean beach, it could be heavily gravel laden, or it could be covered in nothing but sand. There is also very little parking to access this site, so if the parking is full, it may be that way for a while. If you can't get access to this beach then try your luck up where the Moclips River enters the Ocean. I have never had any luck the three times I visited that site, but that doesn't mean you won't either. The good news about Iron Springs is where there is good material and it tends to be of decent size. If I'm staying in Ocean Shores I will hit this site before I hit Damon Point. Not that Damon Point is bad by any means; I've just have some wonderful fortune collecting here and I always hope to repeat the experience.

The agate and chalcedony tend to be clear, yellow, or orange, but I have found some exceptional deep red carnelian here as well. The jasper ranges in the red, green, brown, and yellow tones, but you can also find orbicular jasper. One of the best and brightest pieces of orbicular jasper I've ever found came from this beach. I was going to have it cut and polished for a picture in this book, but I managed to misplace it during a move. Cross your fingers that I find it again and look for it in future updates.

A view of the Pacific Ocean from the collecting area at Iron Springs.

As with many coastal beaches, winter storms tend to pull sand off the shore and expose more of those wonderful gravels we obsess so much over. You can also find fine gravels during the summer too, but just not as likely. Chasing those gravels is all a part of the fun being a rockhound. Be flexible when it comes to beach hounding and be prepared to move to the next beach.

9 Damon Point

A small piece of carnelian typically found at Damon Point.

Land Type: Ocean shoreline
County: Grays Harbor
GPS: N46 55.834' / W124 6.056', 0 ft.
Best Season: Fall and winter during low tide
Land Manager: Washington State—Department of Natural Resources.
Material: Agate, chalcedony, carnelian
Tools: Gem scoop
Vehicle: Any
Accommodations: Camping in area; lodging in Ocean Shores and other nearby coastal towns
Special attractions: The Pacific Ocean
Finding the site: Find your way to Ocean Shores. At the entrance to the city is Point Brown Ave NE. Take this south for 5.2 miles. At this point take a right onto Discovery Ave SE. After 0.2 mile you will see the parking area for the beach.

Rockhounding

This spot is a super popular area with both tourists and locals during the summer, so needless to say it can be quite crowded here at times. The good news is that the best time to collect is during the off-season when the weather downright sucks. Winter storms tend to help clear the beach of sand and expose more gravel and that's what we rockhounds live for. That being said, I have been at this site on a very populated summer day and still managed to find a small handful of agates. I have been to Ocean Shores many times in my life, so I have a lot of memories here. I hope you will have some too.

The agate hunting here is very easy. Just make your way down to the shore and pick a direction to walk. Sometimes the gravel exposures will make this decision for you. Walk the rocky areas and keep your eyes peeled for shiny translucent agates. Having the sun in front of you can help illuminate the agates making them much easier to see. The agate here can be clear, grey, yellow, orange, and rarely a deep carnelian red. Be on the lookout in the gravels for multiple colors of jasper as well and possibly petrified wood. Quartzite (sugar agate) is very common here as well.

There are a few more public beach access points in the area. They tend to be sandy, but now and then you can find some good gravel and that means

Sunset at Damon Point. Just about the only thing to get me to look up when rockhounding.

agates. Do some exploring and if you can make friends with a local and maybe they can let you in on some good spots. You can find some killer deals on oceanfront houses and cabins during the off-season. I know I like to be right on the water as those gravel bars can come and go within hours. If you stay in town I recommend the Oasis Motel. They have always been good to me and I like their funky little rooms. Try to get one on the second floor, as they are the best rooms.

10 Wynoochee River

Our pebble pup, Stinky Dedos, helping out at the Wynoochee River.

Land Type: Forest river

County: Greys Harbor

GPS: Site A: N47 1.326' / W123 41.162', 47 ft. (lower Wynoochee); Site B: N47 26.864' / W123 33.078', 841 ft. (upper Wynoochee)

Best Season: Late spring through fall

Land Manager: Site A: Washington State—Department of Natural Resources; Site B: USFS—Olympic National Forest

Material: Quartzite, epidote, jasper, orbicular jasper, agate

Tools: Gem scoop, geology pick

Vehicle: Any

Accommodations: Camping in Olympic National Forest; lodging in Montesano

Special attractions: Wynoochee Lake; Montasano, hometown of my favorite band the Melvins.

Finding the site: From US 12 west of Montasano take the Devonshire Rd exit and then take a left onto Wynoochee Valley Rd. For Site A travel 4.8 miles until you see a turnout on your left and the gravel below the road. Find a trail that suits you and follow it to the river. For Site B from US 12 take Wynoochee Valley Rd for 33 miles. Pass the turn on the left and continue down NF-22 for 5.7 miles to a campsite on the left-hand side of the road. Park here or near here if it has occupants. There is a trail that runs from the campsite, into the woods, then just before the trail disappears you bushwhack your way down to the river.

Rockhounding

This was a site that was on my radar for a while and then after Ed Lehman suggested I check it out I knew it should be a winner. The drive to the upper Wynoochee is long, but there are huge gravel bars to explore. The scenery is beautiful and there is lots of wildlife running around. The two sites listed are just a couple spots you can access the river. With a good map and a sense of adventure, you should be able to find even more sites to explore.

These jaspers were found in a matter of 20 minutes at the Wynoochee River.

The lower Wynooche is much closer to civilization, is quick to get to, but the gravel is much smaller than what you're going to find in the upper Wynoochee. It's still going to be good material, just better suited for a tumbler. When I visited Site B I was planning on taking NF-22 just a little further to NF-2312 where it crosses the river. From here you can access some huge gravel bars just upriver and around the corner from the bridge. Unfortunately, I ran into a gate just short distance from the turn to the bridge, there were lots of trucks, and some sketchy looking dudes parked at the gate. I backed up, found the campsite on the side of the road, and a trail that leads to the river. If there are no sketchy dudes when you visit, but the gate is locked, you can still walk up the road a few hundred feet to the turn for the bridge. Check Google Earth for an idea of where the large gravel bars are.

While we didn't find any solid orbicular jasper, this splotchy cool guy is getting close.

The prize you are looking for here is orbicular jasper. During our visit, we only found a few small chips of good material and a few more wannabes. I know they can get bigger, but we were here late in the season and didn't have a whole lot of time to explore. In the short amount of time we were

The gravel is smaller but plentiful on the lower Wynoochee River.

there we did find a lot of material. You will find a bunch of red brecciated jasper. Some of it is hard and will take an excellent polish, but a lot of it is porous and well, just a bunch of garbage. Leave that stuff right where you found it. Some of the red jasper can have some green spots, but those tend to be very porous. There was a lot of epidote to be found as well as some unakite. I didn't find any agate, which kind of surprised me. Maybe I was too late in the season and the site had been picked over. Any which way, I hope to return to this area to do some more exploring.

11 Satsop River

Orbicular jasper found in the Satsop River gravels.

Land Type: Forest river
County: Grays Harbor / Mason
GPS: Site A: N46 59.881' / W123 29.416', 16 ft. (Boat launch); Site B: N47 2.651' / W123 31.491', 65 ft.; Site C: N47 18.158' / W123 30.563', 501 ft. (Canyon River)
Best Season: Low water levels
Land Manager: Washington State Parks and Recreation Commission; WSDNR
Material: Agate, Chalcedony, Carnelian, Jasper, Orbicular Jasper, Epidote, Quartz.
Tools: Geology pick, gem-scoop
Vehicle: Any
Accommodations: Camping at Schafer State Park. Lodging in Aberdeen
Special attractions: Aberdeen, hometown of Kurt Cobain
Finding the site: Site A: If headed west from I-5 on US 12 you're going to have to make a U-turn as the highway is split in this area. About 5.5 miles west of Elma, make a U-turn at Monte Brady Rd. Head back east on US 12 for 1.2 miles and then take a right into the boat launch. Park here. At the SW corner of the parking area, you will find a trail leading to the river.

Site B: This at the same spot you would make a U-turn off US 12 for Site A, take Monte Brady Rd. north for 3.8 miles. At some point, Monte Brady Rd turns into Middle Satsop Road. You will see a small pullout of the left before the bridge. Make your way across the bridge, turn around, and then park the correct direction at the pullout. Follow the trail by the bridge down to the water.

Site C: is reached by continuing along Middle Satsop Rd from Site B for another 5.5 miles, so 9.3 miles total from US 12. Take a left onto Boundary Rd and drive 8.4 miles. Take a left onto 73710/Kelley Rd. The bridge here looked like a potential spot for gravel. Continue on Kelley for another 3.2 miles where you continue on NF-2153. Drive 3.2 miles until you get to a bridge crossing Canyon River. Park and make your way to the gravel.

Rockhounding

The Satsop River provides many accessible sites, big gravel bars, and lots of material to choose from. This would make for a great stop on your way to or from ocean beaches or just a great summer day on the river. Plan your visits during low summer water levels. I visited Site A randomly in about 2008 because I was driving home one summer day from a weekend at Ocean Shores and the huge gravel bar was just screaming my name. Years later, I visited in late October and those beautiful big gravel bars were underwater. At least the material is being churned and mixed providing new treasures the following year. The river still has good gravel bars left in the fall and winter, but they are much more difficult to get to without getting very wet.

The agate and chalcedony tend to be in the clear to yellow tone, but I have found a nice piece of bright orange carnelian here. The jasper tends to be in the red and brown tones and sometimes brecciated, but any color could be possible. Keep an eye out for orbicular jasper. Site A is the first place I ever found a piece and I was so excited when I did. It was also the only piece of orbicular I found that day. The epidote tends to be a bright lime green. There quartz is white and massive. The two can form together and make for enjoyable specimens. I have yet to see any petrified wood here, but wouldn't be surprised if some were found. With a little time and enough exploring, you could easily fill a small tumbler with beautiful silicate minerals.

As said before, plan for low water levels, but not too late in the season. These sites are pretty easy to reach from the highway and can get picked over quickly by the summers end. As with most rockhounding sites, wander the gravels far from the road to find the best material. That being said, my very

A view of the bridge from the collecting area at Satsop River, Site A.

first piece of orbicular jasper I ever found was sitting there almost immediately upon reaching the gravel bar, but I just tend to have that kind of fortune when it comes to rocks. For more rockhounding fun you can work your way up to the Wynoochee River. Hey! There's more about that in the previous chapter! Lucky you.

12 Newaukum River

Typical orange carnelian found in the Newaukum River.

Land Type: Valley River
County: Lewis
GPS: Site A: N46 36.486' / W122 50.885', 283 ft. (lower); Site B: N46 37.634' / W122 47.516', 334 ft. (middle); Site C: N46 39.262' / W122 46.800', 383 ft. (upper)
Best Season: Late spring through summer
Land Manager: Washington State—Department of Natural Resources
Material: Agate, chalcedony, carnelian, jasper
Tools: Geology pick, gem scoop
Vehicle: Any
Accommodations: None on site
Special attractions: None
Finding the site: From I-5 take exit 71. Take WA-603/Forest Napavine Rd, then just east of the freeway take a left to keep on E Forest Napavine Rd. Drive 1.6 miles, turn left onto Jackson Hwy. Drive 0.4 mile to N Fork Rd. Take a right and go 0.9 mile. You will see a small pullout to your right by the river. This is Site A. For Site B

continue along N Fork Rd. for another 3.1 miles till you see the big parking area to your right. Site C is another 2.3 miles down N Fork Rd. Cross the bridge and park in the small area on the left side.

Rockhounding

The Newaukum River and its surrounding area have been known for decades for its bountiful supply of excellent carnelian. Unfortunately these days most of the best and most accessible sites are either on private land or have been shut down by timber companies. Not all that long ago, Lucas Creek was once a thriving rockhounding area, but now they have the largest no-rockhounding signs I have ever seen. Finding spots to hunt for carnelian in this area can be difficult, to say the least. I managed to list two sites here. See Site 13 for more information on where the Newaukum joins the Chehalis River.

The prize here is blood-red carnelian and the red from Southwest Washington just can't be beat. It is some of the best natural red carnelian in the world. That being said, the best material is not plentiful. There is a lot of yellow to almost orange agate. You will find a mild amount of nice orange

Some exploring down the Newaukum River will usually result in some treasure.

Sites 12-17

carnelian, but keep your eyes peeled for that deep beautiful red. If mostly buried in mud, they can be tricky to see. Watch out for those icebergs. These ones you definitely want to run into.

Site A was my favorite although there is very limited parking, so if people are there rockhounding or fishing before you get there you may be out of luck for a place to park. It's easy to find your way down to the river from the parking area. I walked far upstream and had some luck. It was very obvious that rockhounds had been there before as there were many foot prints and a couple of dug holes. I don't recommend digging holes and if you do at least have the common courtesy of filling them back in. Site B is a boat launch area with plenty of parking, but there weren't many immediate gravel exposures. This might be a good spot to launch a kayak or inner tube and work your way downstream to Site A. Site C is what I like to call "mostly accessible." What I mean by this is there really isn't a great spot to pull off the road, getting to the river via the bridge is somewhat precarious, and then once in the river there are many spots where you feel like you are right in someone's back yard, which essentially you are although it's perfectly fine for you to be walking the waterway. It just feels odd. Maybe I'm just shy. Anyway, this was not my favorite spot to hunt, although I did find some decent material.

13 Chehalis River

A bright piece of carnelian I found sitting in the tracks or a four-wheeler in the gravel at the Chehalis River.

Land Type: River Gravel Bars
County: Lewis
GPS: Site A: N46 39.065' / W122 58.893', 160 ft. (Alexander Park);
Site B: N46 36.078' / W123 8.785', 225 ft. (Ceres)
Best Season: Late spring through fall
Land Manager: Site A: City of Chehalis (park), WSDNR; Site B; WSDNR
Material: Agate, chalcedony, carnelian, jasper
Tools: Geology pick, gem scoop
Vehicle: Any
Accommodations: Lodging in Chehalis
Special attractions: Rainbow Falls State Park

Finding the site: Site A: From I-5 in Chehalis take exit 77 and head west on SR 6 for 0.9 mile. Take a left onto S Donahoe Rd. Drive 400 feet and take a left onto Riverside Rd W and drive 0.4 mile to the park.

Site B: From I-5 take exit 77 and head west on SR 6 for 9 miles. Take a right onto Ceres Hill Rd. Drive 0.8 mile to White Rd where you will see a parking area.

Rockhounding

The Chehalis River winds its way through excellent carnelian territories and in turn, offers many gravel bars in which to hunt for the elusive fiery-colored silicate. I offer two sites here that have easy access. For less populated and picked over spots I would recommend taking a look at Google Earth, following the Chehalis River, finding gravel deposits, and a road that could possibly get you to them. A kayak would come in handy for this river. There are a few excellent gravel bars inaccessible by car or foot. For you hikers the Willapa Hills Trail can offer many accessible river points. Be sure to respect any private property you may find along your hunt.

A cut banded agate found in the Chehalis River. (Appleyard Collection). Photo by Logon Appleyard.

The prize here as with any carnelian location is the deep red material, but of course, it is rare. There will be some beautiful bright orange material. The majority of what you will find will be clear to yellow tones. The jasper is plentiful. It is mostly in red and brown tones, but other colors can be found as well. As with most agate hunting find the angle of light that works for you. Some like the sun behind them. Some like the sun in front of them. Some like the gravel wet. Some like the gravel dry. Find what works best for you to get the most out of your rockhounding.

The Alexander Park site is a good one for families. After you park decide which gravel bar you want to explore. Taking a look at the park via satellite on Google Maps, which can give you an idea of where you might like to go or you can just try your luck on the many trails leading to the water. Most of the gravel bars will require you to get wet, but on a hot summer day, the river can provide welcome relief from the heat. Site B is more of the same. The first gravel bar is accessible and you will stay dry, but the better gravel is reached by wading through the river. Watch for spawning salmon in the summer. One surprised me in a very shallow part of the river and nearly gave me a heart attack.

14 Doty Hills

Typical size of Augite found in the road cut in the Doty Hills.

Land Type: Forest road cut and a quarry
County: Lewis
GPS: Site A: N46 42.416' / W123 17.273', 1,237 ft. (augite); Site B: N46 41.795' / W123 17.812', 1,845 ft. (zeolites)
Best Season: Any
Land Manager: Washington Department of Natural Resources
Material: Augite, zeolites
Tools: Geology pick, small trowel, three pronged hand held rake
Vehicle: Any
Accommodations: None
Special attractions: None
Finding the site: I'm guessing that most people will be coming from north of this site from cities such as Olympia or Bellingham. Coming north from Vancouver area you would take SR 6, right onto Bunker Creek Rd, right onto Ingalls Rd, and then left onto Lincoln. From the north take exit 88 for US 12 W. Take the highway

west for 3.1 miles then take a right onto Denmark St. SW. Drive 0.9 mile then a right onto James Rd. SW. Drive 1.6 miles to a fork. Take it to the right onto Independence Rd. SW/James Rd. SW. Continue 9.5 miles to Lincoln Creek Rd. Take a right and go for 1.8 miles to a road on your right. Take this for 1.2 miles where you will make a very hard left, drive 0.3 mile to a fork and stay to the left. In 2.3 miles you will see signs of digging on your right. The big pit with the zeolites is another 1.9 miles up the road and will be on your right.

Rockhounding

There are a few deposits of augite throughout the state, but it is not commonly found in crystalline form, and no sites are as easily accessible as the crystals found at the road cut in the Dotty Hills. This site may be limited to how much it may produce and how long we can dig there. If you come to this site be choosy in what you take. You really only need a handful of specimens, as these crystals aren't good for much other than being a specimen of augite from Washington. This would be a good site for kids as it's easy to get to, but remote enough that there's really no traffic.

Augite can easily be collected right out of the dirt at Doty Hills.

Natrolite found in the big quarry in the Doty Hills.

The augite crystals are black, some with a slight green hue. They tend to be somewhat brittle. I like to use a bit of pressure and roll them between my fingers to test for quality. You'll know a good one because the bad ones easily crumble apart. The crystals tend to be on the small side; most being around ¼ inch to ½ inch. The augite found at Cedar Butte in Oregon tends to be a bit larger on average. That being said, my wife found the biggest augite crystal I have ever seen. So there's that.

Once you locate the road cut and park make your way to where people have been digging. The hole is getting quite large and the site is very obvious. I'm honestly not sure why people are digging so much. You can just pick them up off the surface or if it's been picked over just use a small hand rake to stir some up out of the dirt. A small screen might help in this effort. Once you tune your eye to the crystals finding them will be no trouble. Be sure to not let things roll into the road.

After you find enough augite crystals, which should not take long, continue up the hill to the quarry for some zeolites. There were a lot of bullet shells at this site when we visited, so be prepared to not rockhound if there are people shooting. Here you're going to want to have some heavy hammers and

A view of the quarry at Dotty Hills. See those rocks on the ground? They're good for smashing.

You should always rockhound with a friend for safety.

some chisels. Search for boulders and large rocks showing evidence of vugs, or little circular openings in the host rock. It is in these vugs where you will find the zeolites. Bust up some rocks to expose new material. Much of what you will find here will be very small micromount minerals you can only really see with a loop or hand lens. There are, however, some wonderful sprays of natrolite to be found here. I happened to find a really nice vug hidden from the elements on the underside of a large boulder. It was fairly easy to remove, but the natrolite crystals are very fragile and will break if you even look at them wrong. They also can get stabbed under your fingernails, in your fingers, and hands if you're not careful. I learned that the hard way. Take it from Ol' Uncle Lars, and wear some gloves. After some carful and nerve-racking removal I had a couple dozen small, but lovely natrolite crystals. Be careful at this site as we found that we fell down a lot.

15 Green Creek

An agate replaced nautilus found in Green Creek. (Appleyard collection). PHOTO by LOGON APPLEYARD.

Land Type: Heavily forested creek bed
County: Pacific
GPS: N 46 35.155' / W123 35.608', 170 ft.
Best Season: Late spring though summer
Land Manager: Parking area is on private land; creek is Washington State Department of Natural Resources
Material: Chalcedony fossil casts
Tools: Gem scoop
Vehicle: Any
Accommodations: None on site; camping in area; lodging in Raymond.
Special attractions: Willie Keils Grave State Park
Finding the site: From I-5 take exit 77 and head 42.4 miles west on SR 6 toward Pe Ell and Raymond. Take a right onto Green Creek Rd and drive about 1.5 miles till you see a power station and parking area to your right. The trail to the creek is

across the road from the parking area. If coming from Raymond take SR 6 east for 8.7 miles to Green Creek Rd.

Rockhounding

Green Creek offers a unique find for the patient rockhound. The area is well-known for its Oligocene chalcedony fossil casts, but they are not easy to come by and the forest surrounding the creek is lush and thick with all kinds of plants trying to get in your way. We found the devils club was particularly vicious. We also got stabbed and scraped by thorny vines, tripped by hidden tree roots, poked by the ends of broken tree branches, stung by nettles, slipped on more than one wet and rotting log, and I managed to fall into a 3-foot deep hole. Walking the creek is no cakewalk either. The rocks can be slippery and as I mentioned so can the logs. There are spots of loose sand and /or clay that you sink into. I thought I was going to lose my boot a couple of times. It was a tough mission to get away from spots close to the road and well picked. That being said, I found our largest shell cast at the top of the hill leading down to the creek.

The elusive casts can be found in the creek and throughout the river-bank and hillside. The best and most concentrated material is only reached by digging deep. The soil here is wet and full of clay. It would have to be screened out with water and you cannot be doing that in the creek. The clay makes a nasty mess in the water. You also cannot dig into stream banks, your best bet is to cover as much ground as possible and keep your eyes peeled for signs of chalcedony. It would be wise to have your Gold & Fish pamphlet with you at this site.

Now that I've totally studied this site, let's talk about the awesome chalcedony casts that you may find. Most of the chalcedony that filled the voids that once were living creatures is found in clear to yellow/orange tones. We found two clams and one we have yet to identify. Most of the cast found at this site will be clams, but I have also seen nautilus, crab parts, snails, and plant bits. Much more could be hidden there too. Be patient with this site and be happy with what you can find strolling the area. I would hate to see this site get hit hard and get closed down. The GPS and directions take you to the easiest place to access the creek. There are other spots to reach the river that take a much longer walk, but won't be hit by as many rockhounds. Be sure to respect any private property you may encounter especially if the parking status changes at the power station.

This is the face I make when I'm told we have to keep moving down the road for more sites. I could spend all day walking beautiful Green Creek. Photo by Amber Lee Johnson.

16 Grays River

Look for glowing agates in the rain at Grays River.

Land Type: Forested river gravel; old quarry
County: Grays
GPS: Site A: N46 21.964' / W123 33.122', 45 ft. (lower river); Site B: N46 22.834' / W123 30.974', 534 ft. (quarry); Site C: N46 23.499' / W123 28.682', 367 ft. (upper river)
Best Season: Late spring through fall
Land Manager: Washington State—Department of Natural Resources.
Material: Chalcedony, agate, quartz, calcite, jasper
Tools: Geology Pick, gem scoop
Vehicle: Any
Accommodations: None on site
Special attractions: You're not far from the coast
Finding the site: From I-5 in Longview/Kelso, take WA-4 west toward the coast. Head west for about 40 miles then turn right (north) onto Fossil Creek Rd. After just about 0.6 mile you will see river gravels (Site A) and a pullout to your left. Park

here and continue on foot a short distance up the road until you see a short trail leading down to the river. The old quarry (Site B) is another 2.6 miles up the road and on your right. Site C is just about 2.4 more miles up the road from Site B. Right about when you first see the gate blocking the road is where you will want to pull off to the right. There is a trail that will take you down to the river and some gravel bars.

Rockhounding

The Greys River has long been known by rockhounds and fossil collectors for many years. While it does produce some pretty great material, access can be an issue. Marked on the map are two sites you can reach the river quite easily. If you can find a huge gravel bar from Google Earth and want to hack your way through the forest to the river, be my guest. We did very well at the two river sites we visited. The first produced more for us on that day, but the second site looks like a great place to spend a hot summer day just wading through the river for agates. It was raining like crazy during our visit, which it does a lot in this area.

On the river we found quite a bit of agate. Enough so that after a short while of collecting I could start getting picky and only grab the best material. Most of the agate found here is vein agate, so a lot of it is fairly flat and somewhat small. That being said some very large agates can be collected randomly. The agate can range in a wide variety of patterns and colors. We found clear, yellow, grey, blue, and even a couple slightly purple toned agates. A few of the agates displayed patterns and inclusions such as banding, pockets of druzy quartz crystals, moss, very small plumes, and manganese dendrites. I was pretty impressed with the variety and many of the agates we found will cut nice cabochons in the future. We found very little jasper, but the one piece my wife found reminded me very much of Owyhee Picture Jasper from Oregon. There are a lot of rocks that look a lot like orbicular jasper as you're spying the gravels, but it's just garbage.

Site B is an old quarry that is starting to get overgrown. The good stuff is straight back. Ignore the bigger pile to the left. There wasn't anything to be found there. In the dirt and on and around the small pile of rocks at the back of the quarry we found some really cool stuff. There is calcite, chalcedony, and agate loose in the soil and also still trapped in the host rock. You can try smashing some of vuggy rock in hopes of exposing some fresh material. My wife is relentless when it comes to rockhounding and it can be difficult to get her to stop. Now and then her tenacity pays off. On our visit, I found quickly what was there then got back into the truck as it was raining and cold. Amber continued to look around the quarry as I warmed up. Within a few minutes, she came back to the truck with some very interesting green moss agate that I'm sure will make some excellent cabochons and tumbled pieced. I sure do love her. This site is very small, so only take a few specimens, so that everyone can find a piece.

On your way to Site C there will be another quarry on your left. We poked around here for a second and found more of the same material found at Site B, but not quite as much. Truth be told, we didn't look very long. Maybe you'll have better luck. A little tip; be sure to explore some of the logging roads that shoot up and off the main road. The quarry that they use for road gravel in these parts has a lot of agate in it. We found some huge blue agate chucks on the side of the road and lots of tumbler material all over the road. You may find a few big pieces stuck in the middle of the road, but don't be tempted to start digging them not. Not only does it ruin the road, but you may also have a huge log truck come barreling down the hill and they and not to mention the forest service are not going to be happy to find you digging away in the middle of the road.

Purple chalcedony found in the gravel at Grays River.

My wife picking up plentiful agates at Grays River.

I sure do like having my wife with me when rockhounding. Site B, Grays River.

Just up the road from Site C you will notice a gate. If you hike about a mile past this gate and then take the road on your right up the hill you will find another quarry likely full of good material. Maybe even what is filling the logging roads? I'm not sure because it was pouring and we weren't about to walk around in it anymore.

There are fossil concretions found in the area as well. Word is you can sometimes find them in the river, but I did not during my visit. Groups such as NARG sometimes have field trips to this area, so that may be your best bet to find some concretions. Years ago there was a good spot along the highway that produced many excellent crab fossils, but that site is not closed and the state patrol will fine you if caught digging into the road cut.

17 Salmon Creek

It was my buddy's second time rockhounding and he pulled this carnelian beauty out within minutes.

Land Type: Riverbed gravels

County: Lewis

GPS: Site A: N46 24.688' / W122 48.040', 150 ft. (bridge), Site B: N46 23.710' / W122 47.852', 263 ft. (end of road)

Best Season: Late spring through early fall

Land Manager: Washington State—Department of Natural Resources

Material: Agate, carnelian, jasper, iron-siderite nodules (pseudo-coprolites)

Tools: Geology pick

Vehicle: High clearance recommended for the last 2 miles

Accommodations: None on site or nearby

Special attractions: Mount Saint Helens

Finding the site: Driving south on 1-5 take exit 63 toward WA-505 E. Take the highway 5.3 miles to the east then turn right onto Kangas Rd. Drive 1.0 mile to Toledo Salmon Creek Rd. Take a left and stay on this road for 1.4 miles. Here you will cross a bridge and Site A. Site B is another 1.3 miles at the end of the road. The old roads from here all lead down to the creek.

Rockhounding

Salmon Creek is one of the last few publically accessible carnelian locations available in southwestern Washington. Many of the other well-known sites were closed due to over digging, large holes being left, and trash left behind. Let's make sure to keep this area clean and neat just like we found it and it should be. If you must dig into the gravels, be a sweetie and fill in your hole. It is a much easier process than it was to dig it. Also absolutely do not dig next to the creek and create a muddy mess. By being studious and conscious, rockhounds this site can remain open for years to come.

I love this creek. Wading through it and finding deep red carnelian is just a kick in the pants for me. The creek is beautiful, the water is refreshing to walk through, and as much as this site gets visited people seem to keep lulling out excellent carnelian. The deep red carnelian is the most sought after and of course the rarest to find. Much of the agate material here is yellow to orange. Some is solid color, some is banded. The jasper tends to be in the brown and red tones and also seems to get ignored where there is such wonderful carnelian to collect.

There is another collectable material here that has caused quite a lot of arguments over the years because no one truly knows how it came to be. To

Exploring Salmon Creek on a beautiful day.

The "coprolite" commonly found at Salmon Creek. Photo by Amber Lee Johnson.

be blunt, the material looks like ropey poop. For many years it was said to have come from ancient turtles or other creatures. It was sold as this in many rock shops and still is to this day. Somebody finally did some scientific testing on the "turtle turds" and found that it contains no food matter whatsoever and is made out of siderite. The theory was it was pushed out of small holes in the earth resulted in it being so fecal looking. A new study has recently emerged and they now think it might again be fecal matter, but this time coming from giant worms. Whatever they are they sure are fun and you can cause quite a stir with younger friends and relatives by putting an especially gross-looking specimen in your mouth.

18 Washougal River

This little cool guy was trying to hide under sand and rocks. Be sure to check for icebergs at the Washougal River.

Land Type: Riverbed gravels

County: Skamania

GPS: Site A: N45 34.907' / W122 23.906', 16 ft. (Everett and 3rd);
Site B: N45 35.228' / W122 22.470', 22 ft. Site C: N45 37.005' / W122 20.436'(Winkler Creek); Site D: N45 37.276' / W122 16.125', 246 ft. (swimming hole);
Site E: N45 40.380' / W122 9.232', 677 ft. (Dougan Falls)

Best Season: Late spring through fall

Land Manager: Washington State—Department of Natural Resources

Material: Agate, chalcedony, carnelian, jasper, petrified wood

Tools: Geology pick, gem scoop

Vehicle: Any. Discovery Pass required at some upper river locations.

Accommodations: Camping nearby; lodging in Camas

Special attractions: Dougan Falls

Finding the site: I'm going to do the directions here as if you were coming from Vancouver going to each site in alphabetical order. From Vancouver head east on WA-14 E to Camas, for 12 miles. Take exit 12 and after 0.4 mile go forward through the roundabout. Drive 1.0 mile on NW 6th Ave then take a right onto NE Adams St. Drive 0.2 mile then take a left onto NE 3rd Ave. Go another 0.2 mile then take a right onto NE Dallas St. Go yet another 0.2 mile and take a right onto Everett St. The trail leading to the river is at the end of Everett. Find a place to park and then walk. Site B get back to 3rd from Dallas. Drive 1.5 miles on 3rd to N Shepherd Rd. and the park on your right. Park here and find the trail to the river. Site C is reached by taking a left onto N Shepard. Drive 1.1 miles then take a left onto N Washougal River Rd. It's about 2.6 miles to the pullout for Winkler. Site D is another 4.5 miles up Washougal River Rd. The Parking area and trail will be on the right. Dougan Falls is another 9.8 miles up the road.

Rockhounding

The Washougal River is a great place to spend a whole day or just a few hours wandering its many gravel bars. Sometimes it can be difficult to find gravel access at some rivers. This is not one of those rivers. Choose a spot of your liking and if it doesn't pan out, move to another. I would think this would be a great river to do some kayak rockhounding, but I don't own one so I can't say for sure. I do, however, know some people that do very well using a kayak to reach otherwise unattainable gravels.

I have found a lot of various minerals at this river and wouldn't be surprised to find even more. The agate and chalcedony here is found in a variety of colors. I have found clear, grey, yellow, orange, red, and blue so far. The jasper is mostly found in red tones and much of it can be brecciated with quartz or agate. You may also find many other colors including yellow, brown, and green. The few pieces of petrified wood I have from here are excellent. It is very hard and will take a great polish. I have found one piece of chrysocolla here. There are copper deposits in the area so I wouldn't be surprised if other copper minerals such as malachite or azurite could be found. I wouldn't hold my breath for the copper minerals though.

The biggest challenge here is picking a site. I have found great material at every one of them. The two sites downtown (A and B) have a lot of gravel, but you're smack dab in the city, so it can be loud, and absolutely no offence to the town or its fine people, but Camas can smell horrible at times. I have found my largest agates in these locations, but that was just my fortune.

Stinky Dedos keeping a watchful eye on his mama. Notice his cool NW Rockhounds gear.

Art found in nature at the Washougal River.

Sites 18-23

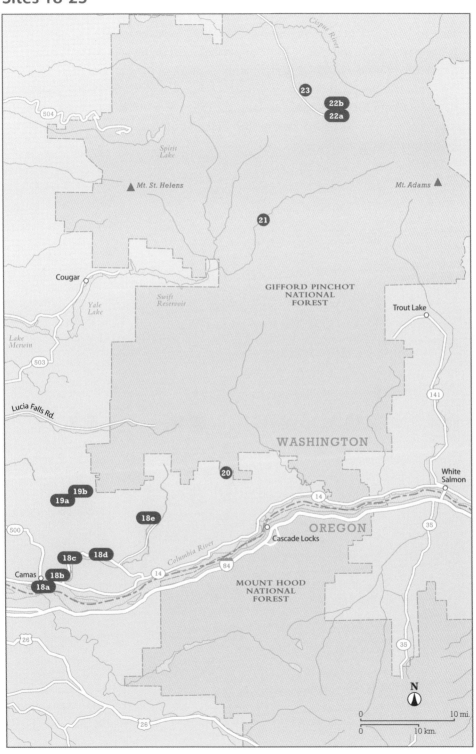

The two upstream sites listed don't have the potential scent problem, but they are both very popular swimming and fishing spots during the summer, especially weekends, and can be quite populated. That being said, at the Winkler Creek site I found a huge agate right at the bottom of the trail and there were a dozen or so people there that day. After a while, I noticed that other people started looking for rocks too. The Dougan Falls site requires a scramble over some large rocks, so it may not be the best site for kids or grandma. Keep going up the river for more access.

19 Rawson Quarry

Find plentiful scolecite at Site A near the Rawson Quarry.

Land Type: Forested road cut; quarry
County: Clark
GPS: Site A: N45 42.784' / W122 20.519', 1,875 ft. (scolecite); Site B: N45 43.103' / W122 19.030', 2,633 ft. (quarry)
Best Season: Any
Land Manager: BLM
Material: Scolecite, micromount minerals
Tools: Geology pick, heavy hammer, chisels
Vehicle: Any
Accommodations: Random dry camping nearby
Special attractions: None
Finding the site: From I-5 in Vancouver, take exit 2 for WA-500 E. Take this for 5.9 miles then turn right onto NE Fourth Plain Blvd (signs for Camas). Drive 1.6 miles then take a left onto NE Ward Rd. Go 4.3 miles then take a right onto NE 139th St.

Go 2.4 miles where you will take a slight left onto Rawson Rd. Continue on Rawson for 5.9 miles where you will see a pullout to your left. Park here and walk to the old logging road across the street. The quarry is another 1.4 miles up the hill.

Rockhounding

Site B, the old Rawson Quarry, has long been known and written up for its micromount minerals. Micromounters are a subset of rockhounds who specialize in very tiny minerals and can handle looking through a loupe for extended periods of time. I do not happen to be one of these people. Staring through a loupe gives me a headache right quick. If you are into tiny minerals then this site may just be for you.

The big drawback is that this site is used for a lot of target practice. To some people it's an old quarry with cool minerals. According to Google Earth, it's a shooting range. I would imagine collecting here on a rainy day may be your best bet as I'm sure the site is filled with shooters on any given nice day, especially on the weekend. With all the shooting that goes on here it's somewhat difficult to get your bearings. There are bullet casings and shot up

All of those white specks are mostly scolecite. It's no trouble finding material at Site B.

debris covering the entire ground at this site. Shot at spray-paint cans created splatters on basalt that at first looked very much like mineral bearing material. Much of the quarry walls are covered with some very strongly opinionated graffiti and it all makes it very difficult to locate good basalt. That being said, I did find some basalt with tiny little amygdules that I couldn't see into because I forgot my loop.

Site A is a spot my sister noticed on our drive in. It was very foggy when we visited, but she could still see white stuff in basalt along what seemed to be an old logging road, so we decided to check it out. The white stuff turned out to be decent zeolite material, most of which is scolecite. The zeolite material is abundant and anyone should be able to walk away with some nice specimens. Be warned though that this site seems to also be used as a target practice spot. There were some My Little Pony dolls here that were involved in a very unfortunate incident. Not as much debris as at the quarry, but a spot people do like to go shooting nonetheless.

Nearby are some other well-known zeolite sites as well, but we had difficulty accessing them. Lawson Lake is known for a zeolite bearing spot in a road cut just a mile or so down Ledbetter Road, but the road was under construction when we visited. I even tried to sneak down it, but there was no getting through. Livingston Quarry is another zeolite collecting spot, but it was very much active when we drove up and we did not want to get in the way of all the hard working folks driving those giant dump trucks. Call them and maybe they will let you in during the weekends or try to hook up with a local rock club that may be able to access sites in the area.

20 Rock Creek

A little piece of chalcedony trying to his in the rocks at Rock Creek.

Land Type: Forest creek
County: Skamania
GPS: N45 44.868' / W121 58.971', 760 ft.
Best Season: Late spring through fall
Land Manager: Washington State—Department of Natural Resources
Material: Agate, chalcedony, calcite, quartz, zeolites
Tools: Geology pick, heavy hammer, chisels
Vehicle: Most
Accommodations: None on site
Special attractions: Bridge of the Gods; Cascade Locks
Finding the site: Coming from Vancouver you can either take WA-14 E (42.5 miles) on the Washington side of the Columbia, or I-84 out of Portland. Either way, make your way east of the Bridge of the Gods and west of Stevenson. Turn left (north) onto SW Rock Creek Dr. and go 0.3 mile. Turn left onto Foster Creek Rd. and drive 0.4 mile where the road will go to the left and turn into Ryan-Allen Rd. Take this 5.7 miles to a bridge. Park on the other end of the bridge to the left.

Rockhounding

When I first moved to the Portland area in 2005, this was one of the first in a handful of locations I tried to check out that were fairly close to the city. I think I first saw it on Billy Bob Tompkins old website. Oh, what a gem that was. You can still find it with some searching through Archive.org and get some great information about northwest sites. This was a time before I had a smartphone or a GPS unit, so I was going off an old Thomas Guide and some very vague directions. I ended up at a creek, but now that I have found the actual site, I was way off. Listed are the correct directions, so you don't get lost like I did.

The Northwest Micro Mineral Study Group sometimes leads trips to this site if you want to learn more about the tiny minerals found here. For the little ones, don't forget to bring a loupe so you can check them out in the field before you drag big chunks home. For the little vugs full of minerals you're going to have to smash a lot of river rock. Search for basalt with tiny empty or filled holes. Give it a good smash and hope you expose vugs filled with tiny mineral specimens. Minerals found here include calcite, chabazite, heulandite, mordenite, quartz (sometimes amethyst), and stilbite. My wife and I also found

My wife searching Rock creek for treasures.

some agate and chalcedony. She found one very small, but very purple piece of chalcedony. We kept trying to find its mother, but she was hiding.

With my first successful visit to Rock Creek, of course, I couldn't have everything work out. Upon arriving to the site we checked things out, got on out river shoes, grabbed the camera and headed to the bridge to see which way we would start. I had forgotten something in the truck and when I got to it I realized I had locked my keys inside. We had zero signal and crossed our fingers someone would drive by. Finally a car came down the hill and I flagged them down. Another car came by shortly and they also pulled over to help. The three different groups of people could not be any more different from each other, but we all had a common bond of enjoying the outdoors. It took us a while, two bent up radio antennas, a lot of swearing, denting my truck door while wedging it open to get the antennas in, but sug nubbitz we got into the truck. I just happened to have two copies of *Rockhounding Oregon* in the truck and gave each group a copy as a thank you for their help. I really wish I could have gotten their names. Thanks, guys.

21 Lewis River

Chalcedony found trying to hide at the Lewis River.

Land Type: Forested river gravels
County: Skamania
GPS: N46 8.686' / W121 53.609', 1,420 ft.
Best Season: Spring through fall
Land Manager: USFS—Gifford Pinchot National Forest
Material: Agate, jasper, zeolites
Tools: Geology pick
Vehicle: Any
Accommodations: Camping throughout area
Special attractions: Mount Saint Helens; The Ape Caves
Finding the site: From I-5 take exit 21 and head east on WA-503/Lewis River Rd for about 46 miles. Take a right onto NF-90 and drive about 1.7 miles to a pullout on your right. Follow the trail back a way around the inner bend of the river.

Rockhounding

The Lewis River is a great spot to hunt if you are visiting the southern Mount Saint Helens area. There is excellent camping right on site and throughout the national forest as well as motels and cabins in the nearby town of Cougar. With many nearby geological attractions such as the Ape Caves and the Forest of Fire, I can say from experience that this is a great place to bring your family for a fun and eventful weekend, especially if you are all rock nerds like my family is.

Finding the site is very easy. There is lots of parking and it's just a short hike down to the river gravels. There should be gravel available all year long, but the best time is when the river is low in the summer and you can access more gravel. The river is very cold, even in the summer, so if you plan on going in be prepared for a bit of a shock. That mountain river water just never warms up. If you are the adventurous type try looking at gravels from Google Earth and see if you can get to them. Some might take some serious bushwhacking to get to, but it will likely pay off with lots of agates and jasper.

Check either side of the bridge for gravel bars at the Lewis River.

Fun for the whole family at the Lewis River.

The agate and chalcedony here are mostly clear, grey, and light yellow, but some light blue can be found. The jasper comes in a plethora of color tones, but as usual in the northwest the most common color found is red. Some of the jasper is brecciated. Check out any river tumbled chunks of basalt showing filled or empty little holes called vugs. Smash them open with a heavy hammer and cross your fingers for some cool zeolites or calcite.

22 East Canyon Creek

Blue agate found at Site B of East Canyon Creek.

Land Type: Creek gravel beds
County: Skamania
GPS: Site A: N46 18.803' / W121 43.936', 2,556 ft.; Site B: N46 19.781' / W121 43.190', 2,290 ft.
Best Season: Summer
Land Manager: USFS—Gifford Pinchot
Material: Agate, jasper
Tools: Geology pick, gem scoop
Vehicle: Any
Accommodations: Camping throughout Gifford Pinchot National Forest
Special attractions: Mt. St. Helens; Mt. Adams; East Canyon Creek Falls
Finding the site: From I-5 take exit 68 just south of Napavine and drive east on US 12 toward Morton/Yakima. After about 48 miles in Randle, you'll want to take a right onto WA-131, which you will follow for 1.0 mile. Then take a slight left onto Cispus Rd, which will eventually turn into NF-23, and drive 21.1 miles to a turn out

which is where you will park for Site B. The gravels are about 0.15 mile down the steep hill. From here to Site A, continue south on NF-23 for 1.4 miles to a bridge. Find a place to park and make your way to the creek below.

Rockhounding

East Canyon Creek was very briefly mentioned in Ream's book *Gems and Minerals of Washington*, but the author did not go into much detail about the site, so I decided to check it out. What I found is that East Canyon Creek is a wonderful, yet remote and physically challenging place to do some good old creek rockhounding. Finding good gravels will require some hiking over large boulders and sometimes over and under fallen trees. Bring your best river shoes along, as it is almost impossible to stay dry at this location. Some of the fallen trees can be absolutely titanic in size and difficult to get around, so be prepared. At one point in the creek my buddy and I had to make a pile of stuff we didn't want getting wet and had to basically swim underneath a monster of a log just to get to some good gravel. We found ourselves very wet and cold, but found some great agates. Being so far out in the woods, make

Grey-blue agate found at Site A of East Canyon Creek.

A first-time rockhound finding beautiful blue agates at East Canyon Creek.

sure to bring a friend, a first-aid kit, and let someone know where you are going and how long you plan on being there. With all the right precautions, this is an undeniably fantastic place to rockhound.

The material found here consists of the usual northwest lineup; agate, jasper and petrified wood. Most of the gemstones found here are from small tumbler sizes to around fist size. The agates are generally grey, light yellow or clear; with some banding and fortification occurring. I have also found a few light blue agates here that are stunningly beautiful. Many of the agates can be found still trapped in their host rock found as large boulders. The jasper can be found in a plethora of colors including green, red, yellow, and brown tones. It is very hard and will take a great polish. Petrified wood was not as abundant as the agate and jasper, but you may find a few hard pieces with some good cellular replacement.

Material is the same at all the sites mentioned here. The only difference between the two sites that I mention is accessibility. At Site A you will find the creek right underneath the road and all you have to do is scamper down to the creek and walk around the boulders looking for gravel deposits. That

Navigate the large boulders for agates at Site A of East Canyon Creek.

being said the boulders are gigantic and can be precarious to get around. Site B is a bit more difficult to reach from the road. Once parked you have to navigate your way 1000 feet downhill through a mostly dry wash that is very steep and filled with loose rocks, massive boulders, and enormous fallen trees. If you can endure this daunting hike you will be rewarded greatly with a gravel bar right at the creek. Follow the creek either way from here to find more gravel deposits. Be sure to do some exploring in the area if time allows and you may find even more access to good gravels. In the style of Ream, I will mention there have been agates reported in Pinto Creek.

Be sure to call the forest service before you trek all the way out to this site. I went to this creek many times in 2015–16. Then the northwest had an unusually snowy winter, and in 2017 the forest roads fell apart resulting in closures and that means no access to the agates. Check ahead to make sure the roads are open.

23 McCoy Creek

Logon had much better experience and weather during his visit to McCoy Creek. Photo by Logon Appleyard.

Land Type: Mountain forest
County: Skamania
GPS: N46 20.482' / W121 47.757', 2,486 ft.
Best Season: Late spring through summer
Land Manager: BLM—Gifford Pinchot National Forest
Material: Pyrite, quartz crystals, gold
Tools: Geology pick, chisel, heavy hammer
Vehicle: 4WD recommended
Accommodations: Camping available in the area
Special attractions: Mt. St. Helens; Mt. Adams
Finding the site: Be aware that some of these roads are often closed during the winter and sometimes can take a long time to repair after winter damage if at all. Be sure to check on road conditions before travel. From I-5 take exit 68 to US 12 E toward Morton/Yakima. Head east some 48 miles and turn right onto WA-131 S. Drive 1.1 miles then take a left onto Cispus Rd. Continue 8 miles and take a

right to continue on Cispus. In 0.9 mile take NF-29 to the left and continue about 9.5 miles to where you will want to start trekking downhill. It's a good idea to have a GPS to help with this one.

Rockhounding

This site can be a tough one. Even Bob Jackson, who first reported on this site, comments in his book that it took him several tries to even locate it. After my visit, I can now see why. Not only is the site in the remote wilderness, but also the parking area is a quarter mile above where you do the collecting. While this might now sound like much, there is no trail leading down to the creek, you kinda have to blaze your own, it is super steep, and can be very slippery in wet weather. The hike back up is even worse. Even knowing this going in I brought along a friend who was very new to rockhounding and had started to have a lot of fun going on trips with me. Let's just say he never asked to go out again after this trip.

During our visit it was pouring rains but we drove all the way there from Portland, Oregon and had to get it done. We basically slid down the hill leading to the creek and not in a fun way, but more in a painful falling down kind of way. We were absolutely drenched when we finally made it to the creek. We poked around for a while, but for the life of me, I could not find where the pyrite was. To be fair it was windy and raining sideways at this point, so it was difficult to concentrate. Jackson reports the pyrite is found in clay seams in altered tuff. I thought I knew what this should look like, but as I said I just could not locate it. I'm not sure if the creek was too high, or if I just looked right over it. We tolerated the weather for as long as we could, but we eventually started the rugged climb back up the hill, which seemed like a thousand times longer that coming down. The upside is on the hike back up I found and picked a few chanterelle mushrooms. There were lots of other mushrooms growing in the area, but I could only identify the chanterelles.

Now you're probably wondering why anybody would ever want to go through the trouble to get to this site just for some "fool's gold?" Well, when Bob Jackson reports that the pyrite found here is the only other pyrite in the state that can compete with the pyrite that is found at the Spruce Ridge Claim (which is one of his claims) near Snoqualmie Pass, you go and you try to find it. At least I did. If you are not familiar with the Spruce Ridge Claim and the fine pyrite and quartz crystals that are found there I highly suggest that you Google that.

Jackson also reports a quartz crystal deposit that can be found in an out-crop about a mile downstream from the pyrite site. You must also trail blaze your way down the riverside through thick forest to get there. I wasn't about to do that. The crystals at the outcrop are reported to be very small, but rare Japan Law Twins (a certain variety of crystal growth) can be found. If you're a masochist, into being wet, and collect small rare quartz growths then this might just be the site for you.

24 Klickitat River

Petrified wood found in the Klickitat River.

Land Type: Forested river
County: Klickitat
GPS: Site A: N45 55.626' / W121 6.323', 784 ft. (Stinson Flats Campground); Site B: N45 59.279' / W121 7.659', 1,026 ft.
Best Season: Late spring through fall
Land Manager: Washington State—Department of Fish and Wildlife
Material: Agate, chalcedony, jasper, petrified wood
Tools: Geology pick, gem scoop
Vehicle: Any. Discover Pass required at Site A
Accommodations: Excellent camping at site and in the area
Special attractions: Cowboy Lake National Wildlife Refuge
Finding the site: Find the turn headed north for Glenwood Hwy on WA-142 between Klickitat and Goldendal. Follow this for about 10 miles to a turn on the left headed downhill to the Stinson Flats Campground. Once to the campground follow the road to the left and find your way to the very end. Park here if you can,

but during the summer the campground might be full and you'll have to park at the day-use area and walk back. At the end of the campground you will find a trail that will take you to the river and a gravel bar. Site B: From the turn to Stinson Flats Campground continue north on Glenwood Hwy for 2.4 miles. Take a right onto Trout Creek Rd and travel 3.4 miles to a fork. Take River Rte Rd. to the left for 0.1 mile and park.

Rockhounding

The Klickitat River is not only fun to say, but it also offers gravels full of excellent silica material. While the material is good, it's not super plentiful, but you'll likely find something. I always have when I've visited. Never a tumbler full, but good material none the less. The downside is the gravel bars that are not the easiest in the world to access. I have listed two sites that are easy to reach and provide a good amount of gravel for you and your family.

For the more adventurous rockhound, I would recommend finding large gravel bars on Google Earth and see if you can blaze your own trail to it. It's a great way to get to gravel that has not been picked over. Be cautious though

Hunt the large gravel bar found at Site A of the Klickitat River.

Sites 24-25

as much of the river is far below the road and a steep hike would be required. There used to be a good spot down near Wahkiacus, but they rebuilt the bridge crossing the river and now there doesn't seem to be anywhere good to pull over. If you can find some parking, this is where I have found most of the petrified wood I've gotten from this river.

The agate and chalcedony will mostly be clear to light yellow, but some blue and grey tones can be found. Much of the agate you will find will have banding. The jasper comes in just about any color, but most commonly you will find it in the red and brown tones. Some will be brecciated. The petrified wood here is excellent and has great cellular replacement. The stuff almost looks like real wood, which I find in plenty. Everything you will find will mostly be on the smaller end, but hard and perfect for tumbling. You may luck out and find a few pieces beastly enough for cutting, but don't hold your breath. Anyway, you cut it the Klickitat River is beautiful and always a pleasure to rockhound.

25 Wood Gulch

Petrified wood and agate found in the Wood Gulch area.

Land Type: High desert
County: Klickitat
GPS: N45 44.424' / W120 12.613', 284 ft.
Best Season: Late spring through fall
Land Manager: BLM/DNR/Private
Material: Petrified wood, agate, chalcedony, carnelian
Tools: Gem scoop
Vehicle: Any
Accommodations: None
Special attractions: The mighty Columbia River
Finding the site: Take WA-14 to Roosevelt. By the convenience store on the west end of town, take Roosevelt Ferry Rd. about a half mile down to the river and start seeing places to pull out. Find a spot, get out, and explore.

Rockhounding

This remote part of Washington is host to some wonderful petrified wood. Not many people are going to make it all the way out here just to find some petrified wood as it is a long drive from anywhere and it's not really on the way to much. The biggest drawback to this site is access. The spot listed here is just about the only place you can get access to. Nearby Rock Creek is accessible and has a lot of gravel, but I was not able to locate anything of interest there. It may have just been the day. Feel free to check it out and if you find anything let me know.

I tried another site just a stone's throw east of this site. It was a very productive dry wash full of great material, but when I was done I was met at my truck by a very upset land owner. He kept cursing me out and the book that gotten me and many others there. I offered to put the stones back, but he wasn't so much concerned about the rocks as he was about people getting hurt by his cattle and suing him. In this day and age, I do not blame him for his concerns. He raises rodeo stock and those are not animals to be trifled with. He said he was going to put up no trespassing signs and hopefully that would alleviate the problem. I'm just glad he didn't call the police on me, although it would have taken them like 9 years to get out there. Please do not collect on this man's land no matter how tempting that dry wash is.

The petrified wood out here is fairly plentiful and very pretty. It can be agatized or opalized, and both varieties usually have excellent cellular replacement. I wasn't able to locate anything much larger than my fist, but that doesn't mean it's not out there. The smaller stuff makes for great tumbler fodder. There are also agates and chalcedony nodules to be found as well. They are mostly clear to yellow, but orange can be found as well. Walk around the sagebrush and keep your eyes peeled for any suspect material and check out everything as there may be mineral icebergs. I wouldn't recommend digging at this site. Just stick to surface collecting. Plenty of material should get churned up for us all after winter freezes.

26 Snake River–West

A small sample of the many things that can be found in the Snake River.

Land Type: High Desert River
County: Benton
GPS: N46 23.372' / W118 40.819', 456 ft.
Best Season: Spring through fall
Land Manager: US Army Corps of Engineers
Material: Quartzite, jasper, granite, conglomerate, porphyry, unakite, garnet
Tools: Geology pick
Vehicle: Any
Accommodations: None
Special attractions: None
Finding the site: From the US 395/I-182 junction in Pasco take I-182 E/US 12 E/ US 395N about 3.5 miles and then take the exit toward Kahlotus. Turn right onto E Lewis St and stay on it for 24 miles. You will see a large building; just before it take a right onto Snake River Rd. and drive 5.1 miles to the Snake River Junction Trailhead.

Rockhounding

(UPDATE) It was brought to my attention at the last minute that picking up rocks on army land is not allowed. I misread the sign that was posted at the site. Instead of yanking this site and offsetting the numbering, I decided to keep it in for inspiration to explore and find a better spot to pick rocks in the area. So sorry for the inconvenience.

At this site the Snake River finally ends its 1,078 mile journey from the Rocky Mountains and becomes one with the mighty Columbia as its largest tributary. At this point a lot of rocks have fallen into the Snake River. Even more, rocks were deposited throughout the area by ancient floods. Needless to say, we found a lot of things here and I think we may have coined a term. A lot of the material we don't know what it is for sure and it requires further testing.

When we first arrived at the site we were up at the parking area by the restrooms. I walked around to scan the area for deposits of rocks. I immediately saw that there were a lot. There was smaller gravel down in the river. There are also larger river tumbled rocks deposited well above the river. Both were productive. What really caught my attention were some rocks way down

Check the hillsides as well as the river gravel at this location of the Snake River.

Sites 26-29

the hill sitting on a cement block. This area once hosted a port and there are remnants of old building and structures, but it was the rocks sitting on it that I truly wondered about. I worked my way down the gravel road leading to the river's edge.

I found many very smooth tumbled stones along the walk and there were even more at the bottom and in the river. The most common thing we found, besides all the granite, were brick red jaspers with even darker red bits in them like a conglomerate. We found many other conglomerates as well. There was a lot of quartzite, as usual, most of it was white. We were finding a sort of porphyry basalt that was very smooth and had a dark green tone to it. Porphyry is sometimes called "writing rock" because of the way the feldspar crystals in the stone line up. Because this material was green and since we were finding it in Washington we dubbed it "Washington Writing Rock." Super nerdy, we know. We found many other things but were not 100 percent sure what they were. I can't even begin to imagine how many varieties of rocks and minerals could be found in the gravel here.

So, I made my way through the sagebrush to find the cement block I saw, picking up stones along the way. Upon arriving at the cement block I noticed the rocks were smashed, and then I noticed they were broken, but bright-red garnets exposed in the break. There was another rockhound here before me! I would have never thought to look for garnet inside the river stones. The garnets were in a very white granite. On the smooth outside of the stone you could see brown to red-brown coloration exposed; these are the garnets. I only found one other rock with the same coloration, and when I smashed it, there was garnet inside. At that moment I wondered where it had eroded out of and how far it had traveled to that place in southeastern Washington.

27 Dixie

Look for rock like this at the road cut east of Dixie. Smash them open to expose fresh vugs.
Photo by Amber Lee Johnson.

Land Type: Road cut
County: Walla Walla
GPS: N46 9.542' / W118 7.895', 1,820 ft.
Best Season: Any
Land Manager: Washington State—Department of Natural Resources
Material: Siderite
Tools: Heavy hammer, chisel
Vehicle: Any
Accommodations: None
Special attractions: Whitman Mission
Finding the site: Take US 12 to Walla Walla. The site is about 13 miles from the last exits for down town Walla Walla. Look for a small parking area on the outside of the curve in the road going left.

Rockhounding

I really wanted to make a joke here. Something; something; ain't whistling Dixie. I just couldn't do it. This was a site mentioned long ago by Cannon (1975), so it's been known about for a long time. The thing is, it's out past Walla Walla. Have you ever been to Walla Walla? I don't think I had before this. I do know I very much enjoy their onions and I'm very happy they ship and I don't have to drive all the way out there for them. It's far from everything.

Other than this site being so far away from everything it is very easy to find and you should quickly walk away with the prize located here; sphärosiderite, a variety of the iron carbonate mineral siderite. The sphärosiderite forms in little black balls in amygdules found in the basalt road cut. Many of the amygdules are filled with more common siderite, and although small, the specimens are quite shiny. There is also some white material filling some of the cavities in the basalt, but I was unable to identify it before print.

The basalt outcrop is easy to reach, but you do have to run across the highway and it can be busy at times. I arrived at this site just before sundown. I managed to snap some quick picture of the site during sunset. There is a

Sunset at the road cut east of Dixie.

lot of basalt just lying there. I preferred to fill my arms up, wait for a pause in the traffic, and then ran them back across the street where I bashed them open with my large hammer while wearing a headlamp. The siderite sparkled brightly in the LED light as the sun disappeared beyond the horizon. I packed a few potentially good pieces in the back of my truck for further investigation at home.

28 Asotin Creek

Land Type: High desert
County: Asotin County
GPS: Site A: N46 20.364' / W117 3.405', 759 ft.; Site B: N46 19.659' / W117 12.333', 1,345 ft.; Site C: N46 18.045' / W117 15.907', 1,622 ft.; Site D: N46 15.730' / W117 17.848', 1,938 ft.
Best Season: Early spring and late fall
Land Manager: Washington State—Department of Natural Resources
Material: Petrified wood
Tools: Geology pick
Vehicle: Any
Accommodations: None on site; lodging in Clarkston and Lewiston
Special attractions: Buffalo Eddy, Nez Perce National Historic Park; Hells Gate State Recreation Area
Finding the site: Take WA-129 south from Clarkston. At 5.6 miles take a right onto Baumeister Rd. The park will be about 0.2 mile up the road. Park here, cross the street and explore the hills. For Site B, continue along the road from Site A for another 3.2 miles, the road will fork here. Take it to the right onto Asotin Creek Rd. Continue another 4.8 miles and take a left to Headgates Park. Park here and explore the hills. Site C is another 11.3 miles up Asotin; parking is on the left and Site D another 3.8 miles from Site C; parking also on the left. Please respect any private property signs should you encounter them.

Rockhounding

I had a very unfortunate incident with my camera involving the accidental pushing of buttons where I lost pictures of many rockhounding sites during my recon for this book. Some of them I managed to get back to and get some replacement shots; some of them I did not. This is, unfortunately, one of the sites I could not return to before press. I also managed to misplace the petrified wood I found here, so my apologies for the lack of site and material photos for this site. I assure you the area is beautiful and the petrified wood is very lovely.

Asotin Creek is a well-known spot in the area to collect petrified wood and isn't a very far drive from Clarkston/Lewiston. The parking is easy and any vehicle can make the trip. The petrified wood found here has great cellular replacement and will take a fine polish. It is found in tones of browns, white, and black. Big chunks for cutting are not abundant so be prepared to be happy with small specimen or tumbling material. The wood is found as float so prepare to do some walking and exploring. This is a popular area with local rockhounds, so try to get further away than most people would for the best chances at finding larger material. That being said, some of my best pieces from popular sites were found smack in the middle of the most searched over spots. Keep your eyes peeled for wood anywhere. There is also some okay jasper in red and brown tones in the area.

This area of Washington can get quite hot in the summer; I mean the area is called Hells Gate for a reason. If the heat is not for you, then try and plan your visit in the colder months or those random cooler summer days. My sister and I could barely stand the heat when we explored this area in early June. I can't even imagine what it is like in July and August.

29 Snake River–East

My prize of the day. It wasn't much, but I was happy to have found it in the Snake River.

Land Type: High desert river
County: Benton
GPS: Site A: N46 22.884' / W117 2.885', 744 ft.; Site B: N46 18.399' / W117 0.788', 783 ft.; Site C: N46 4.861' / W116 58.887', 840 ft.; Site D: N46 4.187' / W117 0.518', 880 ft. (Grande Ronde River)
Best Season: Spring and fall
Land Manager: Washington State—Department of Natural Resources
Material: Agate, chalcedony, jasper, petrified wood
Tools: Geology pick, gem scoop
Vehicle: Any
Accommodations: Lodging in Clarkston and Lewiston
Special attractions: Hells Gate State Park
Finding the site: From Fleshman Way in Clarkston take 5th St./Riverside Drive south for 1.2 miles. The park will be on your left. Site B is another 6.8 miles south at a parking area on the left. Site C is another 19 miles south of Site B. Site D is another 2.7 miles from Site C.

Rockhounding

The Snake River in these parts can get very hot. This is Hells Gate country after all. It got its name for a reason. Avoid summer heats unlike I did when I visited this site with my sister. We could barely stand to be out of the truck for very long. On top of the heat a lot of exposed river gravel in the summer is covered in a white film making it impossible to identify anything. We did manage to find a few decent clean gravel deposits, but not a lot of them. I think spring and fall would be much better hunting times here.

The small amount of gravel we did find had a couple treasures hidden in it. We found a lot of porphyry basalt, granite, quartzite, a few red jaspers, and I managed to find one chalcedony nodule. It wasn't anything to write home about, but I drove all the way out there and I was very happy to find something translucent. I'm sure there are many more rocks and minerals we didn't see all due to the crusty film. I'm sure there is a decent chance for some petrified wood.

Albeit small, we did find some material at all the stops on the Snake River. There was at least a sign that there is material here. Site D is on the Grande

The Snake River provides the rockhound with many collecting opportunities.

Ronde River, which I have had very good luck at finding agates in Oregon. That was not the case here. We had to experience rockhounds on the hunt and we didn't find squat, not even chips of agate or jasper. There was the usual quartzite and porphyry, but not much of anything else. Just because we didn't find much here doesn't mean it's not there. I'm not ready to give up on this part of the Grande Ronde, a river that has treated me so well.

30 Racehorse Creek

Metasequoia fossils found in the landslide at Racehorse Creek.

Land Type: Forest hillside
County: Whatcom
GPS: N48 52.292' / W122 7.030', 1,671 ft.
Best Season: Late spring through summer
Land Manager: Washington State—Department of Natural Resources
Material: Eocene fossils
Tools: Geology pick, chisel
Vehicle: Most
Accommodations: Camping in area
Special attractions: Racehorse Falls
Finding the site: Take WA-524 east from I-5 in Bellingham about 17 miles to Mosquito Lake Rd. Take this south across the river and then turn left onto North Fork Rd. This will eventually become a gravel road. Travel 4.1 miles and turn right at the junction before the bridge over Racehorse Creek. Travel about 2 miles until you hit a gate and park. From here it is a 3.7 mile hike to the trail. Walk 3.1 miles

Sites 30-33

to a fork in the road. Take the sharp left and walk 0.6 mile to a road block. Take the road to the left and hike 300 feet to a switch back to the right next to some logs. Take the path from here to a clear-cut and then follow the trail heading toward a large dead tree. Fossils can be found up or down hill from here.

Rockhounding

In January of 2009, a huge landslide happened near Racehorse Creek exposing a large chunk of the Chuckanut Formation and in turn some superb Eocene plant fossils. I was fortunate enough to have visited when you could still drive very close to the landslide. Unfortunately, as of 2016, the DRN has put up a gate and the site now requires a long hike in. They also dug out the culverts and there are now some seventeen ditches to cross making it inaccessible to bikes even. This is unfortunate for collectors as some of the fossils here can be quite large and now you have to carry them all the way down the hill. The hill where the landslide happened is starting to grow over quite a bit and the exposed fossil bearing rocks are now starting to weather. With hard work and determination the tedious fossil collector can still walk away with some wonderful specimens. It would be a good idea to have a GPS unit or even your smart phone to help guide you in to the waypoint.

While there are many varieties of flora fossils found at Racehorse Creek, most of what you are going to find will be metasequoia and palm fronds. In 2009, shortly after the slide happened, a software writer and amateur geologist found the print of a giant extinct bird, known as Diatryma. It is estimated that the bird was around 7 feet tall and around 350 pounds. Now that's a big bird! Actual vertebrate fossils are extremely rare in the Chukanut Formation, but if you do happen to find one report it right away. For more information about the Racehorse Creek site please see Dave Tucker's blog on the interwebs.

31 Fossil Creek

Smashing rocks at Fossil Creek can expose fossils.

Land Type: Forest creek
County: Whatcom
GPS: N48 54.333' / W121 51.092', 1,363 ft.
Best Season: Spring through fall
Land Manager: Washington State—Department of Natural Resources
Material: Fossils
Tools: Geology pick, heavy hammer
Vehicle: Any
Accommodations: None on site; camping in area
Special attractions: Mt. Baker
Finding the site: Find your way to the town of Glacier on WA-542. Fossil Creek will cross the highway about 5.2 miles down the road. You can park here and find your way to the creek. You can also take NF-3040, which is about 0.5 mile before the site and it will cross Fossil Creek a few times heading up the hill.

Rockhounding

I'm not always the most confident fossil hunter. I think it comes down to me always finding something that looks like it may be something amazing, but just turns out to be nothing at all. I'm the same way with finding lots of pre-petrified wood, also known as wood. With this site, my confidence was much different. It was easy to reach and I found fossils almost immediately. They are right there just waiting for you. Heading farther upstream may yield larger fossil bearing rocks, or you may be about to find the outcrop they are coming from. NF-3040 offers even more access to the creek. Follow it up the hill and it will cross Fossil Creek a few times.

At this site I found mostly belemnites, an extinct order of cephalopods, and a few bivalves. There were many other fossil shells to be found, but I could not confidently identify them. I really need to start hanging out with the North American Research Group more often. They are a NW group that finds, digs, and protects numerous fossil deposits around the northwest states. They are a wealth of fossil information and if you can ever make it to one of their meetings I would highly suggest it.

Walk Fossil Creek up from the bridge to find lots of fossil bearing rock.

Not a lot of rockhounding sites come with their own sign.

Bring a heavy hammer to break open suspect material, and cross your fingers you don't destroy something cool. Perhaps you may want to bring along something to pry lodged fossil bearing rocks from the creek and hillside, such as a geology pick or a paleo pick. In just a very short amount of time you should be able to locate many excellent fossils for your collection.

32 Canyon Creek

Typical fossil leaf found at the quarry above Canyon Creek.

Land Type: Forest hillside
County: Whatcom
GPS: N48 55.273' / W121 57.457', 2,296 ft.
Best Season: Spring through fall
Land Manager: USFS—Mt. Baker-Snoqualmie National Forest
Material: Eocene leaf fossils
Tools: Geology pick, chisel
Vehicle: 4WD suggested
Accommodations: None on site; camping in area
Special attractions: Mt. Baker
Finding the site: Take WA-542 out of Glacier and head about 2.2 miles east. Turn north onto Canyon Creek Rd/NF-31. Drive uphill for 4.5 miles to a fork in the road. Drive 0.2 mile up this road, then take the next fork to the right and the site and parking will be just a few hundred feet up the road.

Rockhounding

The views from this site in the hills above Canyon Creek and the nearby town of Glacier are sweet and spectacular. On a clear day you can see for what seems like forever. The addition of the easy to access fossil bearing rock is a wonderful cherry on top. This site is close to many other fossil sites listed in this book, so if fossils are your jam then you could likely hit them all in one glorious fossil hunting day.

After you wind your way up the hill and locate the small quarry the digging is easy. Like the many other Chuckanut Formation fossil locations (say that ten times fast) you're just splitting rock in the hopes of exposing a layer of various leaves, metasequoia, and palm fronds. You can easily see the fossils showing on the surface of the host rock. Be sure to break open new material for better specimens. A hammer and chisel work best, but paint scrapers and flathead screwdrivers can work in a pinch.

These types of fossil can be easily broken and are very susceptible to the weather. Bring along some thick paper towels or other variety of wrapping to pad the specimens and a shoebox or similar to keep those safe in for the ride

The fossil bearing zone in a quarry above Canyon Creek.

back home. I have made the error of not protecting fossils many times and several of them I worked so hard for never made it home to be put on display on my fossil shelf. Listen to Ol' Uncle Lars and don't make the same mistake. When home keep them inside, in a dry place, and out of direct sunlight. There are many various ways in which you can treat and protect fossils. Try a search on the interwebs for a method that might work for you.

33 Swift Creek / Rainbow Creek

Land Type: Forest creek
County: Whatcom County
GPS: Site A: N48 44.186' / W121 39532', 738 ft. (Swift Creek); Site B: N48 46.012' / W121 39.803', 1,224 ft. (Rainbow Creek)
Best Season: Late spring through summer
Land Manager: BLM
Material: Agate, chalcedony, jasper
Tools: Gem scoop
Vehicle: Any
Accommodations: Camping nearby
Special attractions: Baker Dam; Baker Hot Springs; Pacific Northwest Trail
Finding the site: From Sedro-Woolley take WA-20 E and drive 16.9 miles to between mileposts 82 and 83 where you will take a left onto Baker Lake Rd.
Site A: Take Baker Lake Rd. for another 18.2 miles and then take a left onto NF-1130. After 3.9 miles take a slight right onto NF-1144. In about a half mile you will find the parking area.
Site B: Take Baker Lake Rd. 20.6 miles where you will cross a bridge and find parking on the other side.

Rockhounding

Swift Creek is definitely a place I wish I lived closer to because I would visit it all the time. The surrounding area is absolutely beautiful and worth visiting even if there weren't awesome agates there to find. There is excellent camping and I even hear that the fishing is pretty good. What's not to like about this site? Oh, yeah . . . it's too far from me.

The agate and chalcedony are commonly found in grey and yellow tones, but the really good stuff is a lovely light blue color. These agates make for great tumbling material. When you cut slabs out this and most other blue agates from the NW you will find you lose the color and your agate will end up a mostly grey tone. The material here is best suited for the tumbler. Also be on the lookout for jasper in a wide array of colors, but most commonly red and green.

This creek just like any other is about covering ground, finding gravel, and keeping your eyes peeled for shiny agates and jasper. At this site there are two access points. There's the easy way and the hard way. The easy pickings can be found near the bridge crossing Swift Creek. Just park on the north side of the bridge, find your way down to the creek and follow the gravel. I have done very well here even late in the season. I actually caught the last day when Swift Creek Campground was open once. The hosts were super nice and I had the pick of the place. I found myself a great site right by the water and enjoyed my stay very much.

The hard way isn't even really that hard. It does require an about 1.5 mile round-rip hike, so it's really not that bad. Park your vehicle at the Mt. Baker Hot Springs trail head. The hot springs are a nice place to unwind after a day of collecting. Follow the old abandoned road about 0.25 mile due south. On your left you will find the Swift Creek Trail, which is a part of the Pacific Northwest Trail that stretches from Olympic National Park to Glacier National Park. Could you imagine all the rocks you would find along the way? Follow the trail about a half mile until you reach a clearing and a huge gravel bar. You could also walk the same abandoned road from Park Creek Campground near Site A, but this will be a much longer hike.

A view of Swift Creek gravel from the bridge at Site A. This is the only shot my camera did not erase from that day.

Jackson reports thundereggs being found in the river and at a nearby intersection. I did not find anything I would call a thunderegg in the river, but that doesn't mean they are not there. The eggs found at the intersection sound amazing from Jackson's description, but when I got to the intersection the area had long grown over since it was reported in 1993. It doesn't look like anybody has dug up that way in a very long time. Maybe a tenacious prospector reading this will get inspired and locate the beds again. Be sure to get a hold of me if you do!

34 Loretta Creek / O'Toole Creek

Collect hematite at beautiful Loretta Creek.

Land Type: Forested creek
County: Skagit
GPS: Site A: N48 30.196' / W122 1.242', 112 ft. (Loretta); Site B: N46 30.644' / W121 55.132', 132 ft. (O'Toole)
Best Season: Late spring through fall
Land Manager: Washington State—Department of Natural Resources
Material: Hematite, serpentine, jade
Tools: Geology pick, gems scoop
Vehicle: Any
Accommodations: None on site; camping in area; lodging in nearby towns
Special attractions: Rasar State Park
Finding the site: Headed north on I-5 take exit 231 in Burlington. Take a right onto N Burlington Blvd. Drive 0.4 mile then take a left onto WA-30 E for 3.9 miles. Turn right onto Rhodes Rd. and drive 0.8 mile to a roundabout. Take the exit onto WA-9 S and drive 9.3 miles then take a right onto S Skagit Hwy. Drive 12.7 miles to a pullout on your right just before Loretta Creek. Site B is another 5.1 miles east on S Skagit Hwy.

Sites 34-42

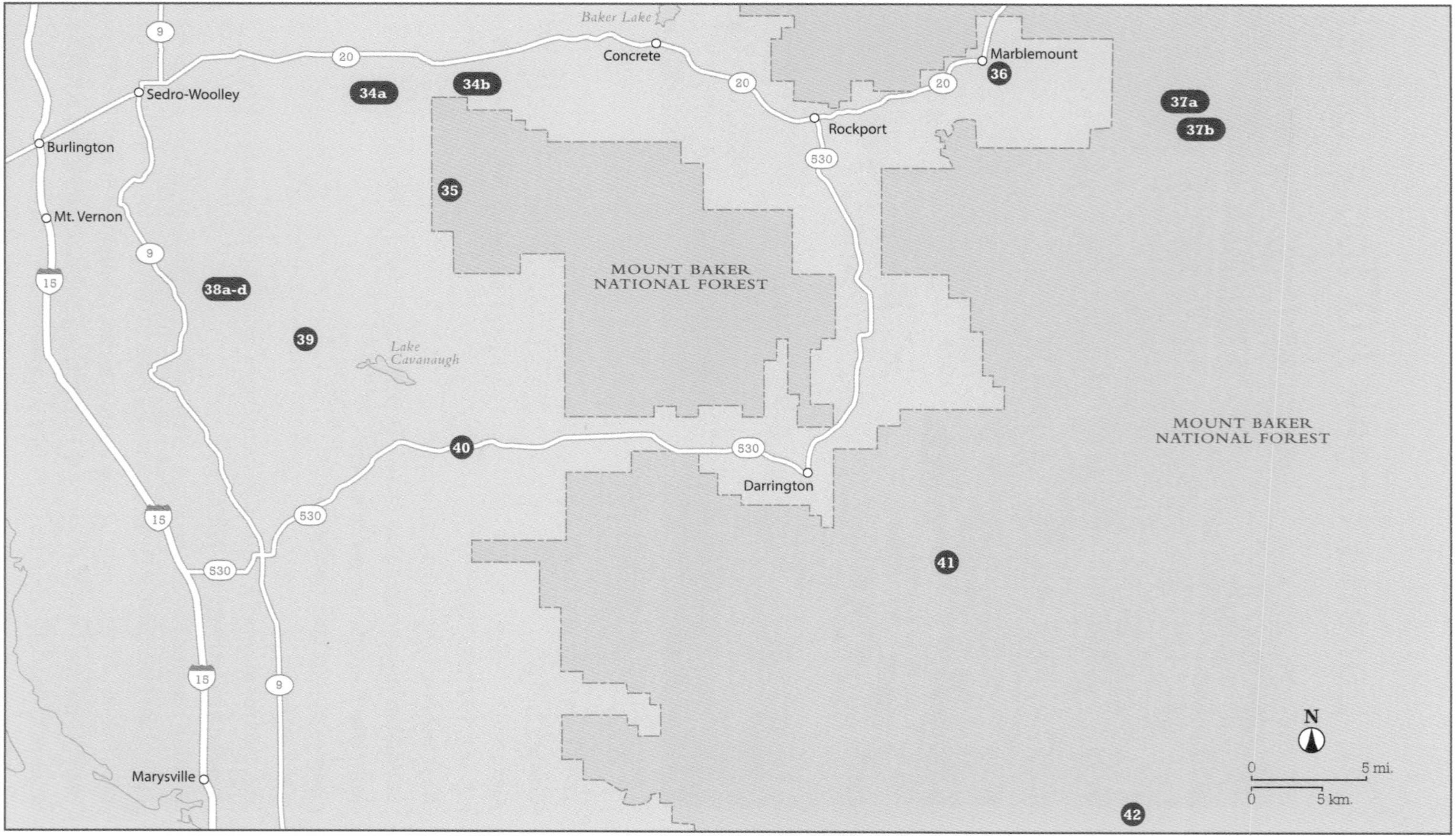

MOUNT BAKER
NATIONAL FOREST

MOUNT BAKER
NATIONAL FOREST

Baker Lake

Lake
Cavanaugh

Marblemount

Rockport

Concrete

Darrington

Sedro-Woolley

Burlington

Mt. Vernon

Marysville

37a

37b

42

36

41

34b

35

34a

40

39

38a-d

20

530

530

530

530

9

9

9

15

15

18

N

0 5 mi.
0 5 km.

Rockhounding

These two sites were a part of the many we visited on our one-day whirlwind tour of Skagit County with Ed Lehman and Bob O'Brien. This was a quick stop as it did not take us long to find what we were there for. This site might not be one you would travel a long distance for, but makes for a nice added stop when exploring the area's many other rockhounding opportunities.

Jade is a well-known material in the Skagit County area. These creeks are no different. If you know what you're looking for you might do well here. I found a lovely green rock in the creek almost immediately. It felt like jade. We put a flashlight to it and it gave off a lovely green glow. I started to get a little excited. Was it finally the jade that has always eluded me? We then gave it the steel knife blade test and it scratched. What I had was a very lovely river tumbled translucent green serpentine. While the piece of serpentine I found was of exceptional quality, my hunt for Washington jade continues. The hematite here is easy to locate. Look for really heavy rocks that a magnet will stick to. Hematite also has a red streak that makes it even more easily identifiable. The hematite is fairly dense and may cut and polish, but I have not tried. My friend Jake is getting tired of all my hematite and hematite-included rocks turning his rock-saw oil bright red. There is a lot of mica-schist in the river that can at times look a lot like hematite, especially when it's dark and rainy.

35 Little Deer Creek

Starburst serpentine found at the outcrop near Little Deer Creek.

Land Type: Forested mountain
County: Skagit
GPS: N48 26.498' / W121 56.900', 3,293 ft.
Best Season: Late spring through fall
Land Manager: USFS—Baker-Snoqualmie National Forest
Material: Starburst serpentine
Tools: Heavy hammers, chisels, pry bar
Vehicle: 4WD
Accommodations: Camping in area
Special attractions: Lake Cavanaugh
Finding the site: From I-5 take exit 208 and take State Hwy. 530 E for 16.8 miles. Take a left onto N Brooks Creek Rd. Drive 0.5 mile to a fork and take it to the left. Travel another 5.8 miles again take the fork to the left. Travel 0.9 mile to yet another fork and take this one to the left as well. Travel 3 miles to yet another fork, but this time you get to take it to the right. At this point is access to Deer Creek

and possibly jade. Continue 4.6 miles to an intersection where you will take a left onto NF-17. Take NF-17 7.2 miles to a large serpentine outcrop on your left. Park to the right.

Rockhounding

This was the last site Ed Lehman and Bob O'Brien took us on our whirlwind tour of Skagit County. We made it just before sunset with just enough time to take some pictures and some samples. On our trek out it got very dark very quickly. To make things worse, a thick blanket of fog rolled in and we could barely see three feet in front of us. The roads in are narrow and steep with huge drop-offs heading down the mountain. Somehow we took a wrong turn and ended way up the mountain. We had a heck of a time turning around. Backing up was terrifying and I'm glad my wife was there with lights and helping direct us. We ended up making it alive, but boy were we rattled from the mountain drive of terror. We do not suggest leaving this site at night.

Once you make it up the winding mountain roads and find the serpentine outcrop the hard part is mostly over. Now you have to bust chunks of

The large outcrop of starburst serpentine near Little Deer Creek.

Starburst serpentine from the Little Deer Creek area.

rock out of the outcrop. We were able to snag a few pieces that others had broken up and left behind. If you want large material for large carvings you're going to need heavy hammers, long pry bars, chisels, some serious elbow grease, and some patience. The big chunks do not come easily or quickly. You're going to have to work for them. If you're a carver and love serpentine then this material is worth the effort.

The serpentine here is a dark green with random sprays of lighter material. We had a long discussion about what could be mixed with the serpentine, but only came up with some theories and nothing conclusive. Whatever it is, it is beautiful. Immediately walking up to the outcrop I thought it looked a lot like seraphinite, a gem quality variety of clinochlore used in the jewelry market. Ed tells me it's slightly translucent when slabbed, but he has yet to try and cut a cabochon from it. Serpentine is a little soft to make long-lasting jewelry from, but I have seen it before and you might want to give it a try. Remember though, serpentine has an asbestos in it. Caution should always be used when cutting or grinding this material. Face masks are essential if any dust is going to occur. You should be okay digging the material, but if you're worried bring a face mask just in case.

36 Jordon Creek

Chrysocolla all found by my wife at Jordon Creek. The rest of us didn't find much of anything.

Land Type: Forest creek
County: Skagit
GPS: N48 31.110' / W121 25.154', 384 ft.
Best Season: Late spring through fall
Land Manager: Skagit County
Material: Garnierite, chrysoprase
Tools: Heavy hammer, geology pick
Vehicle: Any
Accommodations: None on site. Camping in area
Special attractions: Northern Cascades National Park
Finding the site: From I-5 take WA-20 to Marblemount. Continue on WA-20 east of Marblemount for about a mile to Cascade River Rd. Take a right and follow it for 0.7 mile. Take another right onto Rockport Cascade Rd and travel 0.7 mile past the fish hatchery to a bridge over the creek where you can park at either side.

Rockhounding

Jordon Creek provides the rockhound the rare chance at finding some chrysoprase. Chrysoprase is a variety of chalcedony colored green by traces of nickel. It is a beautiful apple-green color and can rival the well-known Australian

A view of Jordon Creek from the bridge that crosses it at the site.

variety. Good job, Washington, good job. If you're lucky enough to find a big piece some excellent cabochons can be made. Ed Lehman and Bob O'Brien brought me to this site also showed me a wonderful cabochon they made from this chrysoprase. Now, I have been in the mineral and jewelry business for quite a while now. If someone were to have shown me this cabochon in the shop I would have sworn it was from "down under."

The site was easy to find and Ed showed me how to attack this site. You want to look for orange rusty-looking rocks. This is oxidized nickel and very much helps find potential chrysoprase. To find the good stuff you're going to have to bust open a lot of rock. Then after all your hard work you're going to see that inside most of these rusty rocks you're going to find another nickel ore called garnierite. It will be light green to grey in color and isn't of much interest to the lapidary. Ed tells me it's not easy to find the good chrysoprase and it usually forms in thing seams not big enough to cut. That being said, my wife found a lot of excellent slab and cab-worthy material just poking out of the ground near the road. For most, finding good chrysoprase will consist of hard work, patience, and some good fortune. Get further up the creek to get away from where most people go. I have seen reports of the same material being found on nearby Cultus Mountain. It might be worth checking out.

A little side note: there are two dogs that live at the property near the bridge. Let's just say that they are *very* friendly. Especially if you have a dog like we did. Our little boy Papillion proved to be very popular with the two large white dogs. Oh, and as friendly as the two dogs are, they do not like people on bikes. I thought a person riding by was going to get it. Good for them they were fast.

37 Cascade River

Typical soapstone found way above the waters of the Cascade River.

Land Type: Mountain forest
County: Skagit
GPS: Site A: N48 29.950' / W121 14.500', 1,605 ft.; Site B: N48 28.863' / W121 13.490', 1,981 ft.
Best Season: Spring through fall
Land Manager: USFS—Mt. Baker National Forest
Material: Soapstone
Tools: Saw, chisel, hammer
Vehicle: 4WD suggested
Accommodations: None on site; camping in area
Special attractions: None
Finding the site: Take WA-20 to Marblemount. At the east end of town, the highway turns to the north. Go forward across the bridge on Cascade River Rd. Take Cascade for 11 miles to an opening in the forest on your left. This is Site A. Continue up the hill for another 1.5 miles to reach Site B.

Rockhounding

Soapstone has been used as a carving material for thousands of years. People thought the talc-schist had been used by Vikings and Native Americans to make everything from cooking utensils and smoking pipes to statuary of deities. In the right artistic hands this metamorphic rock can be turned into absolute beauty from a block cut from the earth. Soapstone tends to have an asbestos content, so extreme caution should be used when carving or sanding this material.

Collecting soapstone is a rather simple process. The best method to get uniform sizes is to cut it out of the outcrop with a saw, yes a regular old wood saw. The soft soapstone is easily cut and does not need traditional diamond saws like a lot of lapidary material. Find a spot in an outcrop that looks solid and start cutting away. It's easier to star off where someone else has finished, but you can go about it as you will. Should you decide to saw, please wear a proper mask to keep dust out of your lungs.

You can also use traditional hard rock mining techniques. A good hammer and chisel will work to free material from outcrops. This method will not

Look for signs of where people were cutting out soapstone.

Ed Lehman checking on a soapstone deposit close to the Cascade River.

This was some material Ed Lehman picked up for a fellow club member of his. She loves to carve and this piece was nice and solid.

yield uniform pieces like sawing does, but I know artists who like to work with what they have and a uniform piece is just too simple. You are the master of your carvings. Find the method that works best for you.

Like a cloudy overcast Pacific Northwest sky, the soapstone form this locality tends to be grey to greenish-grey. Soapstone is easily identified in the field. It tends to have a very "soapy" feeling, hence its name. It also scratches with a finger nail. Site A showed a few signs of digging, but it looked like it happened a while ago. Site B has been worked a bit more and has the telltale signs of soapstone harvesting; big blocky cuts out of the hillside outcrop.

38 Walker Valley

A quartz stalactite found by Ed Lehman at the big pit at Walker Valley. (Lehman Collection)

Land Type: Open quarry; forested hillsides
County: Skagit
GPS: Site A: N48 22.346' / W122 10.009', 567 ft. (bellow quarry); Site B: N48 22.350' / W122 9.750', 799 ft. (Junior); Site C: N48 22.364' / W122 9.935', 657 ft. (quarry); Site D: N48 22.586' / W122 9.652', 863 ft. (old quarry trailhead)
Best Season: Late spring through summer
Land Manager: Washington State Mineral Council lease via the Washington State Department of Natural Resources
Material: Quartz geodes, amethyst, agate, chalcedony, calcite, goethite, hematite, pyrite, rutile, siderite
Tools: Heavy hammer, chisel, gad, pry bar
Vehicle: Any. Discovery Pass required
Accommodations: Camping in area
Special attractions: Lake Challenge

Finding the site: From I-5 take exit 226 and head east on WA-536 E /E Kincaid St. Continue 0.1 mile forward onto Broad St. After 0.5 mile take a left onto S 15th St. Drive anther 0.4 mile then take a right onto E Division St. Take Division 3.2 miles to WA-9 S. Take a right on WA-9 S and travel 3 miles. Take a left onto Walker Valley Rd and continue 2.2 miles. Then take a right onto Peter Burns Rd. Drive through the ORV setup area and start up the hill. At 1.5 miles will be a pullout to the left and Site A. Continue along Peter Burns 0.3 mile to a spur road leading up a hill. You will notice a very weathered WSMC sign here. Continue up the hill for about a half mile to a gate. Park here but do not block the gate. See text for directions to Sites B through D.

Rockhounding

Walker Valley was one of the first sites that really caught my attention years ago when I was a young sprouting rockhound. I first read about it in Lanny Ream's book *Gems and Minerals of Washington*. The idea of digging amethyst geodes in my home state kinda blew my mind at the time. It would take close to 20 years before I finally made it there to dig. I know, it's crazy, but that's just how it works out sometimes. I didn't find my giant amethyst geode I was hoping for, but I did, however, get certain sense of closure. I finally made it to Walker Valley.

The Walker Valley collecting area was first taken notice of in the late 60' when the area was quarried for road fill. Since then it has always been a popular rockhounding site. There is now a very large pit to dig in and many other spots in the area have been found as well over the years. The Junior Pit was discovered by a junior rockhound from a local club when nature called and he wandered off into the woods. He came back with a big chunk of agate and now it is a popular dig site with a sign above the digs commemo- rating the junior rockhound that found it. The Walker Valley collecting area is 20 acres and under lease from the state by the Washington State Mineral Council. The sales from their maps are what keeps this site open and avail- able to generations of rockhounds. If you don't have a copy of the WSMC maps I highly suggest you get one. If you do have one, then get another one for a friend.

I have now visited this site many times and let me tell you there is a lot to be had. I have mentioned the amethyst geodes. They aren't very common anymore, but they do surface now and then. Clear quartz geodes are not uncommon. There is a lot of agate much of it is banded and can be a nice light to medium blue color. The old Fly by Night blue agate claim is nearby, but I'm told it is now on private property owned by the farmer down the road. Other minerals found here include calcite, goethite, hematite, pyrite, rutile, and siderite. They can all be found alone or in combinations with or inside of each other. Some nice quartz and chalcedony with siderite or goethite inclusions have been retrieved here.

I'll do a quick rundown of the digging options I have listed. The first area, Site A, is a road cut just under the large quarry. Many geodes have been found here. You can see signs of them in boulders that have come down or pried out. Ed tells me you should look for teardrop shapes that are the same color of the host rock. These are the geodes and agate. If you look up to the top of this site you will see what looks like a cave. Ed tells me that this was a giant geode pocket that never mineralized. You can see that people have somehow climbed into it and have been digging. I would not recommend this.

Site B is the Junior Agate Seam and is just before and on the right side of the gate. Follow the trail up the hill. You will notice digging in the outcrop. The spot with the sign is just to the right of this that has produced some large agate. This is a big agate seam; some spots can get quite thick. You can work

Goethite "roses" commonly found in the big pit at Walker Valley.

material out of the outcrop or you can try to find some float. Ed says getting under some of the talus may produce things that have long been covered. The agate is mostly white and grey but can be light blue at times. Some cut pieces here can look like a stormy Washington day at the beach.

Site C is the big pit. It is just past the locked gate and to the left. This site has been dug for a very long time, but still produces. We found a few small quartz geodes, some bits of light-colored amethyst geodes, goethite "flowers," and a bit of calcite. This area is hard rock mining and in not easy. It requires heavy hammers, gads, chisels, and pry bars. There is even a rockhounding invention called a Walker Valley Wedge. They are made from truck springs and beaten into cracks in the basalt to help widen the crack and take out large chunks. They are soft so they bend and follow cracks that may otherwise break brittle tools. When you arrive to the big pit there are actually two of them. The one to the left is still producing, but not much has been coming out of the right side, but things can change. There is also a dig just below the hill to the very right of the quarry. Go up and over the small hill and you will see signs of digging.

A view of the giant geode found at Site A of Walker Valley.

NW Rockhound, Brad Kernodle, checking the debris at Walker Valley for missed treasure.
PHOTO by DAVID MCFARLAND

Site D is an old quarry way up top and requires the most hiking of all the sites. It is also hard rock mining, so you have to hike in your equipment, not to mention anything might you bring back down. The GPS gets you to the trail head, which is the second turnout up the road from the gate. Take the old road/trail 0.3 mile up to the digs. Some beautiful agate and quartz have come out of this site. Ed tells me there is a guy who has posted up somewhere up on the mountain and claims that he has a claim and even puts up bogus claim markers on land that is and has been leased by the WSMC for a while now. If anyone approaches you saying you are on a claim, you are not.

The Walker Valley rockhounding area is a pleasure to visit and know that so many generations of rockhounds have been enjoying the vast bounty of this site. If you have not visited this site yet, I would suggest putting it on your rockhounding Washington list toward the top.

39 Pilchuck Creek

The granite found here at Pilchuck Creek and also all over Washington.

Land Type: Forest creek
County: Skagit
GPS: N48 20.542' / W122 5.129', 823 ft.
Best Season: Late spring through fall
Land Manager: Washington State—Department of Natural Resources
Material: Jade, agate, jasper, granite
Tools: Gem scoop, geology pick
Vehicle: Any
Accommodations: Camping nearby; lodging in Mt. Vernon
Special attractions: Big Lake, Walker Valley
Finding the site: You will want to end up on Cavanaugh Rd, which can be reached coming north or south from WA-9. From WA-538 in Mt. Vernon take WA-9 south for about 5.5 miles to Cavanaugh Rd. Take a left and drive about 7.5 miles to a pullout on your right. The creek is easily accessed from here.

Rockhounding

This site is absolutely lovely. The creek is beautiful and my wife and I spent the last part of a day rockhounding and playing in the gravel. The sun set, the moon came out and it was huge. It shone so brightly on the river we just couldn't leave. It was a very whimsical evening for us and I'll never forget it. All the sappy stuff aside, Pilchuck Creek isn't a bad place to find some rocks.

Jade is found here, but as you will read in other chapters I'm horrible at finding jade and I certainly did not find any here. This is a jade country and Ed Lehman tells me it's there, so darn it I'm going to say it's there. This creek also runs through rhodonite country as well, but that's not always easy to find in the river either. The outside is oxidized black due to the manganese content in rhodonite and you have to try to chip of just enough of the rind to expose the pink inside, but not totally destroy it into pieces. What we did find was light blue agate and chalcedony, but not whole lot and nothing was very large. It was also pretty late in the season and I'm sure people were here rockhounding before us. There was jasper, and of course, it was mostly in red tones,

Stinky Dedos helping out at Pilchuck Creek. He's great at sniffing out the good ones.

but a few yellows and tans showed up too. There is a ton of salt and pepper granite here, so have at it.

While this might not be a site that you would drive a very long way just for the site itself; it is totally worth it to spend the latter half of a day playing in the river after breaking a sweat up at Walker Valley. If you live in the area, then I highly suggest this be one over your summertime stops.

40 Deer Creek

Cross the footbridge above Deer Creek in Oso to get to the gravel and possibly jade.

Land Type: River gravels
County: Snohomish
GPS: N48 16.293' / W121 55.873', 183 ft. (big gravel bar)
Best Season: Late spring
Land Manager: Washington State—Department of Natural Resources
Material: Jade
Tools: Geology pick, gem scoop
Vehicle: Any
Accommodations: None on site; camping in the area
Special attractions: Lookout Mountain
Finding the site: From I-5 take exit 208 and head east on SH 530 for about 15.4 miles. Take a left onto Lake Cavanaugh Rd. In a few hundred feet and after the curve in the road you will see the bridge to your right and a pullout to your left. Do not block the driveway. Cross the bridge and find the trail down to the creek.

Rockhounding

Deer Creek, a tributary to the Stilaguamish River, has long been known as a producer of fine Washington nephrite jade. The creek runs through an area that is not only known for jade, but also grossular garnet, jasper, and rhodonite. There is also a lot of white massive quartz and granite to be found, but who actually collects that stuff? Not me.

With this site being so easily accessible and well known the pickings are going to be slim the later it gets into the season. You're going to want to get to the creek just after the water levels drop and new gravel is exposed. The bigger gravel bar will be across the creek to the north when you reach the creek, but you'll have to ford your way across. You may be able to find some good pullouts and gravel bars along the Stilaguamish River and try your luck there. On low water level days you could likely walk your way south to the river and right to some gravel bars.

Even if you get to the creek early enough you really have to know what you are looking for. What you are after is a fine green jade. The problem is just about every other rock in this creek is green too. Along with that jade can also sometimes form a brown crust on the outside hiding the colorful jade in the center. Many people take suspect pieces home to cut on a rock saw to check for color. We tried the smashing with a hammer in the field test and the results all came back negative. This is good, as I would be really bummed out if I destroyed a beautiful piece of jade. The jade here often comes in a botryoidal form. Botryoidal translates to "grape like" and many minerals can be found in this form. Look for bubbly stones as these may likely be the jade you are looking for. Jade will not scratch with a steel pocket knife.

Jade hunters seem to be a rockhound breed of their own. They tend to mostly or only hunt jade and can be downright secretive about their collecting areas. They also know exactly what to look for. As a guy who hunts mostly agates and jaspers in his travels I must admit that I do not have the jade eye, but after trying to find some I highly respect those who do. If you don't have the jade eye I wouldn't really recommend driving a super long way to just hunt at this site as you will likely walk away with nothing just as we did. It's a good thing the surrounding countryside is beautiful and there are more obtainable minerals further down the highway.

41 Sweetwater

Banded calcite found at the Sweetwater site.

Land Type: Mountain forest
County: Snohomish
GPS: N48 11.861' / W121 28.039', 2,097 ft. (parking bellow deposit)
Best Season: Spring through fall
Land Manager: USFS—Wenatchee National Forest
Material: Banded calcite (onyx)
Tools: Geology pick
Vehicle: Any
Accommodations: Camping in area
Special attractions: None
Finding the site: From 1-5 take WA-530 to Darrington. From Darrington take the Mountain Loop Hwy south and drive 8.9 miles then take a left onto N Sauk River Rd. for 0.4 mile, take a hard right and continue for 2.6 miles to NF-22. Take a right here and drive 1.7 miles. You will see a small creek on your right and the deposit.

Rockhounding

The term onyx gets thrown around a lot in the mineral world quite a lot. It can refer to black chalcedony, which is usually dyed, but very popular in the jewelry industry. It can refer to banded white and brown agate that is often used for cameo carvings also used for jewelry. The onyx found at this site is a variety of travertine calcite or calcite marble. Calcite is pretty soft and doesn't make for great jewelry, though in my many years of selling rocks and jewelry I have seen some things set that you would never think of, so go ahead try if you like. You are the Frankie Avalon of your cabochon. The travertine will dissolve in even light acids. We put a piece in some vinegar, it immediately began to bubble, and after a short while, it was gone. It will dissolve almost immediately in muriatic acid. Although fun to watch I don't recommend playing with acid, at least the variety that turns litmus red.

Collecting the onyx here is very easy. It is found as veins and can be botryoidal. This material has orange-brown and white banding and is easily identified. The little stream and the surrounding hillside it is flowing out of

Checking out little holes in the wall for treasure. There was none there.

are littered with the stuff. It did not take us long to accumulate more than enough, which wasn't that much. This material is just a small specimen grade and it shouldn't be difficult to pick out a few great pieces. This isn't a particularly large collecting site, so take only a few specimens. Let's make sure there is plenty of material for all future rockhounds to come.

I must give a special thank you to NW Rockhound member Maria Santa Cruz. During our visit to this site, my truck decided to mysteriously not want to start. We were far from the main road and losing light and our phones were about to die. My wife, Amber, shot a text out to Maria as she knew she lived somewhat close. Late that night after a great dinner, drinks, and what we are pretty sure was a Sasquatch encounter; the local sheriff found us and helped us to get out of there. Thank you very much, Maria, for your help. The kindness of our rockhound group is yet another of the many reasons I love being a member of NW Rockhounds.

42 Sloan Creek

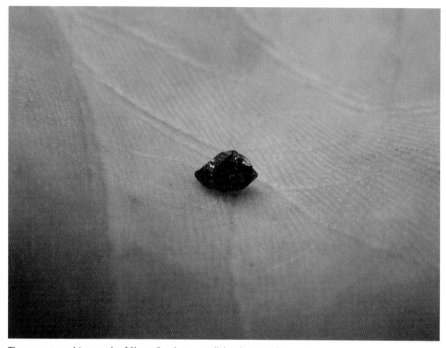

The garnets at this stretch of Sloan Creek are small, but boy are they red.

Land Type: Forest creek
County: Snohomish
GPS: N48 01.530' / W121 17.171', 2,468 ft.
Best Season: Late spring through summer
Land Manager: BLM—Wenatchee National Forest
Material: Garnet
Tools: Gold pan, various small mesh screens
Vehicle: Any
Accommodations: Camping in area
Special attractions: Big Four Ice Caves
Finding the site: From Darrington take the Mountain Loop Hwy about 16 miles to Bedal. Take a left onto NF-47 for about 9 miles where you will take a right at the fork and about a half mile down you will find the parking area. Be sure to have your Northwest Forest Pass with you. Find your way to the creek across the bridge.

Rockhounding

Some excellent garnets have been found at upper Sloan Creek. I have even heard a rumor that some of the garnets have star asteration (an optical gem phenomenon), but I have never seen one for myself so I cannot verify this claim. The huge bummer in the road leading up to the better garnets is washed out. If you really want to give it a shot, you will need to go on about a 9 mile round-trip hike. There have been claims staked up there so if you do make the trek be sure to watch out for claim markers and respect the claim holders.

The garnet you will find at the lower section of Sloan Creek is mostly tiny in size, but can be very bright glowing red. We honestly did not spent a whole lot of time at this site, as we were pressed for time, but we did find very quickly that if we poked around in the sand surround the river rock we would eventually pop out some bright garnets. I did not pan or screen at this site, but I'm very certain both methods would help find a fair amount of garnet. If you have been to the Heather Lake garnet site, this site is much less productive than there and may prove disappointing.

My wife and pup trying to figure out where the large garnets are in Sloan Creek.

I wouldn't travel a long distance for this site, but that being said, if you are in or close to the Darrington area this site is absolutely lovely and the rock-hounding isn't so bad either. It would be a great family or couples destination to have a picnic lunch and some gem hunting. Be sure to pack out what you pack in and keep this spot beautiful and accessible for the next generations. If you have time to explore the area you might likely find more garnet deposits or loose crystals in the creeks.

Fairly close to Sloan Creek are a couple spots worth mentioning, but are difficult to get to. One is Gothic Peak. It is a very long and arduous 5-mile hike up to the top of the mountain, but once there if you have enough energy left over you can find quartz crystals and clusters. The WSMC has lead trips to this site in the past, so check their event calendar. Also nearby is Vesper Peak, which is known for its wonderful grossular garnets. The site is under claim and the claim holders sometimes grant permission to collect, but they have to like and trust you first, so permission is not easily granted.

Check the sand deposits at Sloan Creek for garnet.

43 Skykomish River

Land Type: Forest river
County: Snohomish
GPS: N47 51.598' / W121 49.127', 102 ft.
Best Season: Spring through fall
Land Manager: Washington State—Department of Natural Resources
Material: Agate, jasper, petrified wood
Tools: Geology pick, gem scoop
Vehicle: Any. Discovery Pass required
Accommodations: Camping nearby; lodging in Sultan
Special attractions: Wallace Falls State Park
Finding the site: Take US 2 to the middle of Sultan. Take Mann Rd. south for 0.3 mile across the bridge. On your left you will see a short drive leading to a parking area. Park here and follow the trail under the bridge, through the woods, and to the gravel bars.

Rockhounding

It's funny I wasn't planning on having this river as a site. I was having a tough day doing recon for the book. Little did I know at the time I had just found a sweet piece of moss agate at Stubbs Hill. I didn't realize until I got home several days later. I had otherwise been getting skunked that day; following some bad information and I was getting grumpy. I always find some peace near water so I decided to make my way down to the river just before sunset. I sat for a while and thought about this book, my wife back at home, and where I would go next. It was a warm day, so I decided to wade in the river. I hadn't remembered ever reading anything about the Skykomish, so I wasn't particularly looking for anything, but what do you know I started to find some silicates.

At first, I noticed the typical white quartzite you find everywhere. I could go out to my yard, dig a random hole, and it's highly likely that I'll pull out quartzite. The stuff is everywhere. All the quartzite; all the time. Pretty soon I started noticing other things. First I found what was a dark red and brown agate. It looked like it could have been from a colorful piece of wood, but it was too small to be sure. It was pretty whatever it was. Shortly thereafter I found a very nice piece of tan petrified wood and then right after that some red jasper. I was pleasantly surprised and wanted to keep hunting, but the sun

Sites 43-48

was going down and I still needed to get back to my car and back on the road. I would like to spend a long summer day walking the abundant gravel at this site. I'm sure there are access points along the Skykomish River for even more gravel. Take an adventure and see if you're as fortunate as I was.

I could swear up and down that I brought my camera down to the river, took shots of the river, and the couple of cool guys I found. I distinctly remember standing in the river taking a photograph. By the time I got home there were only shots from sites earlier that day and the sites I visited in the following days. I also found out when I got home and started looking up the river that there is a spot that produces funky blobby round calcite concretions, but no word on where. I would very much like to find that spot.

44 Stubbs Hill / Cedar Ponds

The moss agate I tripped over at Stubbs Hill when I lost the trail for a minute.

Land Type: Forest; creek bed
County: Snohomish
GPS: Site A: N47 48.554' / W121 49.492', 597 ft. (Youngs Creek); Site B: N47 48.419' / W121 49.352', 622 ft. (Stubbs Hill Parking); Site C: N47 48.935' / W121 46.504', 1,288 ft. (Cedar Ponds)
Best Season: Late spring through fall
Land Manager: Site A and B: Washington Department of Natural Resources; Site C: Campbell Global Resources
Material: Jasper, agate, moss agate, quartz crystals
Tools: Geology pick, paleo pick, shovel
Vehicle: Any. Discover Pass required
Accommodations: None at sites. Lodging in Sultan
Special attractions: Al Borlan Park
Finding the site: From US 2 in Monroe take WA-203/N Lewis St. south for 1.2 miles. Take a left onto Ben Howard Rd and continue for 6.3 miles. Turn right onto Cedar Ponds Rd. Zero out your odometer here. The road turns sharply to the right at about a mile then take the right fork 0.3 mile from the sharp turn. At about 3.3 miles in you will see a gated road to your right and a bridge. Park here and don't block the gate. Make your way down to the creek. Site D is reached by walking the

road past the blue gate here for 1.3 miles until you see a gravel pit on the left. Site B is another 0.1 mile up the road. You will see a blue gate on your left. Park by the gate, but don't block it. See the Rockhounding section for trail directions. Site C parking is another 1.4 miles up the road. Park by the gate, but don't block it.

Rockhounding

I'll start with Cedar Ponds, Site C. This site has long been known for producing small clear quartz crystals and even a few amethyst tipped scepters. I've never seen anything out of here over a couple inches, but the quality of the crystals is nice and they are worth collecting if you are into quartz crystals. In the past, the site used to be open fully to the public. The area the quartz is found and the road leading in is now run by Campbell Global Resources and casual hiking on the land is not permitted and can result in a fine. The good news is you can purchase a day pass or a yearlong pass from the company and not get fined if found without a permit. Visit their website for more information on obtaining said permit. If you don't plan on visiting the quartz spot more than once in a year, the fee may not be worth it to you. One last thing, be careful where you park. There are lots of signs put up by the locals who are also reported to not be so friendly. For sure do not go down to the lake.

I don't have a GPS waypoint for Site A because I left my GPS unit and my phone back in my truck when I visited. It is nearly impossible to find the exact spot on Google Earth because the road isn't on the map and the site is covered by thick forest. I'm going to use the directions provided by the Maplewood Rock & Gem Club, which is what I used to find the spot. Find the parking spot and do not block the gate. This is an old logging road that isn't used anymore and parts are becoming very overgrown. You will have to go through some plants at a few points. Follow the old road uphill. After 0.2 mile the road will take a sharp turn to the right. Ignore the overgrown spur road on your right. You will cross a small creek before heading uphill again. Along the way you will pass two spur roads on your left. The second spur almost looks like the main road, but isn't. Bushwhack to the right and continue on the road. At about 0.6 mile the road will make a sharp right turn again and start heading uphill. Follow the road until you get to a flat spot just before the road turns to the left. Along the way is a pull out that may seem like the spot, but it's a little more uphill. You will find a very faint arrow made of rocks pointing to the trail on the right hand side that leads down to the digging area.

It may be a bit of a hike in, but I found some great material. I, in fact, tripped over my best piece, a nice chunk of red and green moss agate, when I momentarily lost the trail on my way down the hill to the dig site. I later found out from Ed Lehman, the man who found this spot, that the rock I found is from where he used to dig at the top of the hill back in the day. He hadn't seen any in years and said I was very fortunate to have found such a large chunk. After you locate the collecting area you can go about finding material in two ways. Your first option is to hike around the steep fern-covered hill and hope you trip over a fantastic piece like I did, but that's not likely. Your second option is to dig. Find a worked on hole or start one of your own and check each piece for red. A spray bottle would come in handy here. The moss agate I found I at first thought was just a decent-sized chunk of dirty red jasper. I threw it into my pack to photograph in better light later and went on with my day. It wasn't until I got home and scrubbed all the dirt off did I notice that is was some pretty sweet moss agate that my friend Jake Rankin (@nwrockdogs) cut some sweet slabs and cabs out of. The jasper here is also very pretty and tends to be very bright red with patches of agate in it. A word of warning: there is a

The jasper digs at Stubbs Hill.

Youngs Creek is a producer of jasper and gold in the Stubbs Hill area.

VERY steep hill at the bottom of the digging area. Watch your dogs, children, and yourself around this spot as it is a long way down that very steep hillside.

Site B is a lovely creek you can walk and search for tumbled jasper, agate and chalcedony. This creek is also popular with gold panners and I could see lots of evidence of them being there. The gold here is reported as fine. For more information about the gold in the area please refer to Romaine's, *Gold Panning in the Pacific Northwest*, put out by Falcon Guides. I mostly found red brecciated jasper in the river, but it was late in the collecting season and I'm sure it had been picked over all summer. Prepare to do some long creek walking for better material. Jasper can also be found in an old quarry and along the road a 1.3 miles up the road (Youngs Creek Truck Trail) past the gate by the bridge. I had little light left in my collecting day so I decided to not hike up the road. There are also reports of fossil leaves and marcasite included petrified wood. Consult the WSMC maps for more information about these sites and many more places to check out. Also if you're up to it and have the time do some prospecting in this area as it is well known for its mineral riches.

45 Heather Lake

My little frog buddy helping me screen for garnets in Lake Creek near Heather Lake.

Land Type: Forest creek
County: Chelan
GPS: N47 51.578' / W121 5.536', 2,768 ft.
Best Season: Summer through fall
Land Manager: USFS—Okanogan-Wenatchee
Material: Garnet, schist, quartz
Tools: Shovel, screens
Vehicle: Most
Accommodations: Camping throughout the Okanogan-Wenatchee National Forest
Special attractions: Mount Pilchuck State Park
Finding the site: From Granite Falls take N Alder north out of town. This will turn into Mountain Loop Hwy. Drive for 12 miles and then take a right onto Mt. Pilchuck Rd. Follow this for about 1.5 miles until you reach the Heather Lake Trailhead. You will need a Northwest Forest Pass to park here.

Rockhounding

Lake Creek flowing from Heather Lake has long been known for its beautiful almandine garnets. The gemstones here are small, about the size of a peppercorn, but they are plentiful and if you're lucky you may find a couple the size of a pea. My favorite specimens were garnet still imbedded in the host schist. The garnets are almost too small to tumble, but if you visit this site several times and save all your largest stones, you may be able to put a polish on a small batch in a 3-lb. tumbler. If you are very good at making teeny-tiny cabochons these garnets would be great for a project, otherwise, these gorgeous red gemstones are best used as specimens of Washington garnets. I like to keep them in cute tiny antique jars. Be aware if you plan on visiting this site as the trailhead may not be accessible November through May, but that's okay because the best collecting times are after May.

For this trip, you are going to want to have a good shovel. It can be collapsible or not, just make sure that it is well built and sturdy. Most people like to bring screens to this locality, but I can see how people can do well just sifting through handful after handful of gravel. If you have access to a screen or can build one yourself, the best size of screen to use is ⅛ inch. Even though it adds more weight to your hike, an additional ¼ inch screen can be very helpful to stack on top of the ⅛ inch screen to remove the larger junk stone and also to find bigger garnets.

The drive into this site is mostly paved. The last few miles are a somewhat bumpy gravel road, but any vehicle with decent clearance should be able to make it in. There is also a 1.3–2 mile hike in. When you park at the Heather Lake Trailhead make sure to have your Forest Pass with you or pay the day fee at the trail head. The Forest Service also asks that you register the people in your party who will use the trail. The hike in is relatively low in elevation change, but the trail goes uphill both ways. You will also have to take into consideration that you have to hike your screens and shovels in. Luckily, even if you find a million garnets, they won't weigh too much to pack out.

From the trailhead parking hike about 1.3 miles or until you start to see the creek below you. From here to about another mile down the trail find a way down to the creek. Many people have different places they prefer to look. Some like to start looking immediately. Some swear the garnets are bigger the further in you go. Some say it doesn't matter. I'll let you come up with your own hypothesis.

Look for plentiful garnets in Lake Creek near Heather Lake.

Once you find yourself breathing heavily and are finally in the waters of the chilly creek, catch your breath and start thinking like a gold miner. The garnets are going to be found mostly behind large boulders, the inside curves of the creek, and in generally slow areas of the creek. Once you find one or more of these spots, you will want to begin screening out the gravel. Get the large rocks out of the way and then start shoveling loads into your screen. It can be very helpful to find a nice flat rock to screen on, but just about anywhere will do. Screen out the sand and start picking garnets. I'll tell you that a nice bright sun helps to locate the red glowing gems.

For those of you that find yourself not wanting to leave this site, bring home a gallon bag of screened concentrated sand. I had fun couple of weeks picking garnets out of the sand on my porch when I had that need to collect, but couldn't get out of the city. I will warn you though; a gallon-sized storage bag full of wet garnet sand is quite a bit heavier than you may think. Be prepared for a weighted hike out if you try this method.

46 Geology Adventures

Land Type: Multiple
County: Multiple
GPS: N47 21.768' / W122 1.413', 563 ft. (Johnson's Home and Garden, Maple Valley, WA)
Best Season: Varies
Land Manager: Private
Material: Amber, quartz crystals, fluorescent minerals, garnet, fossils, and much more
Tools: Varies
Vehicle: Varies
Accommodations: Camping or lodging available at locations
Special attractions: Varies
Finding the site: www.geologyadventures.com

Rockhounding

Geology Adventures is a fee-based field trip company owned and operated by Bob Jackson. Bob is a well-known northwest geologist, rockhound, mine owner and has worked as a collector for many prominent museums. He has had access to several collecting opportunities both in the Pacific Northwest and around the world. His website, www.geologyadventures.com, offers many single and multiple day trips around Washington. Bob also has a yearly open house where he offers for sale many of the beautiful specimens he has collected in his travels. There are also classes available for both beginners and seasoned diggers to learn more about northwest rockhounding and geology. After you have gone on all of Bob's NW adventures, get ready to drool over his international trips. They are on my bucket list for sure.

I found Bob's website many moons ago when I had my first little rock shop in a gas station I ran and lived at in Tumwater, WA. I would spend hours on his website drooling over his collection and digging opportunities. One night while having dinner with my father I mentioned Bob and all of his awesome mining claims. Long story short, it turns out that my father and Bob are friends. Not through rocks, but through the hardware store my father owns. I must admit that I fanboy a bit whenever Bob shows up at any of my father's events. If you ever meet me be sure to ask me about the "gneiss story."

The only trip of Bob's I've personally been on was his amber dig. The location is owned and maintained by the city of Renton, but Bob has special permission to lead trips to the site. Amber is only found at handful of locations in North America and near Tiger Mountain in King County just happens to be one of them. The 45-million year old amber is very small and most pieces are only suited for a specimen collection, but what a cool specimen; Washington amber! Very rarely will you find a piece big enough to do any sort of lapidary work on. Most of the amber found will be yellow-orange, but the rare piece of blue amber can be obtained. Once at the site digging is very easy and only involves cutting slices out of a hill with a butter knife. You will also have the opportunity to collect leaf fossils and if you're really lucky clam or snail fossils.

Since I don't want to just go giving away all of Bob's sites; I listed the GPS location as my father's hardware store in Maple Valley. Here you can purchase many rockhounding supplies including the awesome yellow buckets featuring my last name you see me out rockhounding with. On rockhounding trips I lead, people who know me, very well know better than to bring one of those awful orange buckets from a box store I won't name, but I'm sure you can figure out. I will not stand for them being in my truck. No way.

47 Hansen Creek

Land Type: Forested mountain
County: King
GPS: Site A (parking): N47 22.710' / W121 30.966', 2,459 ft.; Site B (bottom of dig site): N45 23.093' / W121 30.319', 2,752 ft.
Best Season: Late spring through late fall
Land Manager: BLM—Mt. Baker-Snoqualmie National Forest
Material: Quartz crystals, amethyst crystals, pyrite
Tools: Paleo pick, shovel, screen, trowel, rake, screwdriver
Vehicle: Any
Accommodations: Camping in area; lodging in North Bend and Cle Elum
Special attractions: Twin Peaks filming locations in North Bend & Snoqualmie; Snoqualmie Falls; Summit at Snoqualmie
Finding the site: Whether heading east from Seattle or west from Ellensburg take I-90 to either exit 45 or 47. It's nice because if you miss one, you can take the next. Exit 47 gets you closer to the dig site quicker. Exit 45 will take you past most of the camping sites if you want to set up camp first. My directions will be from exit 47. Take the exit and head south to a T in the road. This is Tinkham Rd. Take a right onto the gravel road and drive 1.3 miles to a fork. Take the fork to the left onto NF-1550 and begin to drive uphill for another 1.6 miles to a big curve in the road headed to the right. You will likely see people parked here, but if not look for the large boulders blocking a road on the outside (left) of the curve. This is where the trail begins. From here hike about a mile or so until you start to see holes dug into the hillside. My GPS reading is an educated guess as I can never get my GPS to work in all the trees. From here you can go up just about anywhere. There is a claim way up the hill, but most people don't make it that far up. However, if you are a mountain goat type, be sure to keep an eye out for claim markers and signs.

Rockhounding

I have been rockhounding at this site now for many years and I have to say it is one of my favorites. Not only is the material easy to find, but sometimes you will find rare crystal formations. If you cannot hike over a mile to the site, go up hill form there, and have enough energy to dig and screen, then this may not be the site for you. Otherwise, this is a very fun and productive rockhounding site that families visit often.

There is excellent camping all along Tinkham Road. There is a developed campground and lots of sites just off the road. I have my favorite sites to camp and I'm sure you'll find one of your own. One thing to keep in mind is this area is very close to populated cities and visited by a lot of people. One year I was camped at my favorite spot and spend the day digging. When I returned to my campsite I found that I had been robbed. It wasn't a whole lot of stuff, or very valuable, but it still hurt and irritated me to know that someone would do that especially way out there. Keep your valuables in a safe place.

Once you reach the site you will find that there is quartz sparkling on the ground everywhere. You will know you have found the site when it starts to look like you are in a forested war zone. This site has been hit hard for a great many years. Bob Jackson reports when he first started visiting this site many years ago there were just a few holes scattered about. Nowadays there are holes everywhere in the hillside and it's almost sad to see. That being said the holes in the hill are nowhere near as deep or a damaging as say gold or copper mines and even though some people have undercut trees and their root systems I'm certain that long after we're gone Mother Nature will have no trouble reclaiming this area. She has already started on the trail up. You used to be able to drive all the way up, but now the road is blocked and spots on the trail are almost overgrown. It is now hard to imagine that I got my truck up that road with how narrow it has become. The awesome thing about having the road blocked now is that idiots cannot bring their garbage and dump it up there. Before the road was blocked not only did the site look like a war zone, but it looked like a war zone in a dump.

The quartz crystals here can be simply stunning. Most are around an inch long, give or take, but some can reach up to 6 inches. Most are clear, some being water clear. What people are coming here year after year is the amethyst. The amethyst occurs mostly in the tips of the crystals and can be especially nice when in a scepter-shaped crystal. I like the scepters even when they don't have amethyst. You may also find inclusions in the quartz, including but not limited to chlorite, pyrite, and enhydros. Enhydros are tiny gas bubbles trapped inside certain minerals that contain ancient water. They are not the easiest to spot in the quartz, but they are amazing when you do. Examine your haul carefully after you get them home and cleaned. A quick internet search can tell you the many ways people clean quartz crystals. Also, check all your crystals against a piece of white paper for light amethyst or inclusions that otherwise may be easily missed.

Some of the better quartz and amethyst points we have found at Hansen Creek over the years.
PHOTO by AMBER LEE JOHNSON.

Finding quartz at Hansen Creek is very easy and just about everyone should walk away with some treasure. There are two main methods of attack here. First, you can just walk around and check for crystals in and around piles of dirt left by previous rockhounds. Some people are only looking for large and /or purple and simply discard perfectly good smaller crystals. The other method, and my personal favorite, is digging and screening. Find a spot that looks as if no one has dug and go straight in. To get all the crystals you will need to screen your dirt. Some people use ½ inch mesh, some people use ¼ inch. I like the latter as I like to keep all the little clear crystals to use as jewelry points. I find that two people working a hole together is much more productive, but you must first agree on how you are going to split the treasure you find. Digging a hole by yourself works perfectly well too. Do be careful to not get yourself in a precarious situation by tunneling too far back and having a bunch of overburden above you. People have died at this site having the roof

This is where you begin your hike up the hill to the crystals at Hansen Creek.

collapse on them. In fact, there is a memorial for someone way up the hill. No mineral is worth your life. Use your most important tool out here; your brain. Also, remember to please try to fill in any holes you may dig.

High above Site B is an area known as Upper Hansen Creek or Butterfly to locals. In all the years I have dug this site I have never been up there. It is hard rock mining and I much prefer to dig and screen, so I've never gone. I have a vague idea where it is, but I don't want to get anyone lost trying to find it. Members of NW Rockhounds on Facebook sometimes lead trips up there, so if you really want to bang on some rocks become a member and check out the events page. It's a great group to be a part of.

A fun note about the area: a scene from the movie *Harry and the Henderson's* was filmed on the road leading to parking area for the dig site. Watch the movie and see if you can figure out where. They may have chosen this area to shoot in for good reason as there have been a lot of Bigfoot sightings and reports that have happened here over the years. One quiet and eerie night while camping here many years ago I heard some very strange noises and knocking off in the distance. I want to believe. . . .

48 Denny Creek

Grossular garnet commonly found at the Denny Creek collecting area.

Land Type: Forested mountain creek
County: King
GPS: N47 25.637' / W121 27.139', 2,830 ft.
Best Season: Spring through summer
Land Manager: USFS—Wenatchee National Forest
Material: Quartz crystals, epidote, garnet, hematite
Tools: Geology pick, heavy hammer, chisel
Vehicle: Any. NW Forest Pass required
Accommodations: Camping throughout the Wenatchee National Forest
Special attractions: Twin Peaks filming locations in North Bend & Snoqualmie; Snoqualmie Falls; Summit at Snoqualmie
Finding the site: From I-5 take exit 47. Go to the north side of the Freeway and take NF-9034 west for 0.3 mile. Take a left on NF-5800 and drive 2.3 miles. Take a left onto FS 5830 and drive 0.3 mile to the Denny Creek Trailhead. If the parking area at the trailhead is packed, then there is another parking lot back the way you came in.

Rockhounding

I must start off by telling you there is an area just above the collecting spot that is locally known as Dead Rockhound Gulch. I almost didn't include this site because of its reputation and the tragedies that have happened there, but a lot of people already know about this area, dig there, and I hope that my writings will help educate some people to the unfortunate events that have happened in the area and hopefully prevent future tragedy. The gulch is an area that was once known for its rare and beautiful raspberry scepter quartz crystals. The deposit has long been dug out, but unfortunately many unwise and unexperienced rockhounds have met their death trying to access the precarious area the quartz was once found. Absolutely no rock is worth your life. Do not even consider going very far up the wash above the collecting area. Just a few hundred feet up the hill you will begin to see where large boulders are sitting precariously high above the wash. Do not get under them. The old collecting area is even more treacherous. Do not go exploring up there. Just don't. Also don't be a show off around the many waterfalls here. A lot of people have fallen off them and gotten seriously injured.

Now that I've scared you half to death, let's talk about the many awesome minerals you can find in the safe and productive area of Denny Creek. The main attraction to this area is the rare raspberry quartz and while some people have found them as float, it is an extremely rare occurrence. Don't hold your breath for any of those. What you will find is lots of garnets, small quartz crystals and clusters, epidote, and hematite. The garnet is of the grossular variety and is brown to reddish-brown tones at this site. They don't really get much bigger than a half inch at best. Most are very small and it would be difficult to find anything worth faceting. Most of the garnet is of specimen grade only. The quartz is plentiful but finding pieces with crystal faces can be difficult. Inspect quartz poking out of the dirt as I could be an iceberg and be hiding the crystal below the dirt. The epidote is found both massive and in crystal form. The massive formation epidote will be found as a bright green stone, mostly tumbled in the creek. The crystals are lovely little sprays of dark green epidote. It is very brittle so try to keep it in matrix. I did find a few loose crystals in the talus, but most of them broke easily in my hand. Only a couple survived the trip back. The hematite found here is very reflective and not hard to miss. Most of the loose hematite you will find will be small and flakey, but with due diligence, some pieces up to an inch or so can be found. You will also see streaks of it in the host rock. My favorite pieces from this site

The path to doom. Please do not go far up that wash. They call it "Dead Rockhound Gulch" for a reason.

were specimens that featured a bit of everything on them. A couple of these should satisfy any rockhounds craving.

I wouldn't recommend digging here. Surface collecting is OK, but don't go digging up any holes. There is plenty of material that can be found on the surface. A heavy hammer will help with breaking up any chunks of matrix with crystals exposed or signs of mineralization. You may find more crystals inside the matrix, but mostly you'll want to trim down specimens to a manageable size. Remember you have to hike everything back out to the parking area.

49 Greenwater

A cut piece of black and red agate from Greenwater. (Appleyard collection). PHOTO by LOGON APPLEYARD.

Land Type: Mountain forest
County: Pierce
GPS: Site A: N47 6.069' / W121 31.319', 3,582 ft. (red and black agate) Site B: N47 6.140' / W121 31.092', 3,693 ft. (opalized wood and opal)
Best Season: Late spring through fall
Land Manager: USFS—Mt. Baker-Snoqualmie National Forest
Material: Agate, jasper, opal, petrified wood
Tools: Pick, shovel
Vehicle: 4WD
Accommodations: Lots of camping in the area
Special attractions: Mt. Rainer, Gorge Cliffs
Finding the site: Take WA-410 to just southeast of Greenwater. Turn onto NF-70 and drive 5.8 miles. Take a right onto FS-72 ad drive 0.7 mile to NF-7220 at the fork. Take this for 0.3 mile to the next fork; continue to the left. Drive 0.8 mile to another fork and take it to the right. Continue for 0.9 mile until you see a spur road

on your left. Take this a few hundred feet and start looking for signs of digging on either side of the road and find a safe place to pull out. This is Site A. To get to Site B continue up the hill from the turn for Site A for 0.3 mile to a pullout on your left. Park here and then follow the trail leading north for about 0.3 mile to where the forest opens up at the top of the hill. The diggings are downhill to your right headed east.

Rockhounding

The Greenwater area is well known by rockhounds, but is still ripe with collecting opportunities. The variety is huge and new material is being found all the time. It is an area worth exploring and getting away from the main digs. This is a site that WSMC leads field trips to and I highly suggest attending one if you have the chance. Also please see the WSMC maps for more information about this site. I just marked a couple sites here. Get on the roads back there and do some exploring. Keep an eye peeled for landslides and tape markers on the side of the road. Sometimes people mark the trail leading to a site.

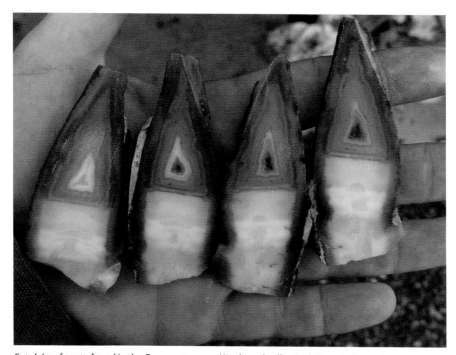

Cut slabs of agate found in the Greenwater area. (Appleyard collection). Photo by Logon Appleyard.

The digging area at Site B of Greenwater.

The most well-known material from this area is the agate, especially the red and black agate that is popular with local lapidaries. The agate and chalcedony here can range in a wide variety of colors and patterns and more is being found. My favorite is a wonderful icy-blue banded seam agate. You lose the blue coloring when cut into slabs, but there is potential for iris effect. In the general, Greenwater area the now popular Tahoma Agate is found. There is a claim on the majority of the land that it is found, but pieces can be recovered from the surrounding hillside. For the sake of the claim holders, I did not include a GPS for the Tahoma Agate. For that one, you're going to have to do your homework.

The opal is common or potch opal and like the agate can come in a wide variety of colors. Again my favorite is a blue opal. My friends were pretty tight-lipped about the blue opal spot and I don't blame them. When you write books such as this one people stop telling you their spots. Woe is me. The jasper here, you guessed it, also comes in a wide variety of colors. Most common are red and /or green, but many other tones can be found as well. The petrified wood can be agatized or opalized. It has great cellular

Sites 49-54

Digging a hole just to see where it goes. Site A, Greenwater.

replacement and comes mostly in brown tones. It's a virtual silicate shopping mall at Greenwater.

Most surface material, especially on areas close to any road here, has long been picked up. You may find some decent small chunks around dug pits. Some people only want the big stuff. Bring a good pick and shovel to dig a hole and find your own cache of agates. Some material may need to be broken free from host rock, so have a good heavy hammer and some chisels to help break it loose. If you want to make sure and get every last piece in the hole then bring a ½ inch screen. Maybe your tumbler is hungry.

50 Pyramid Creek

Little quartz crystals found at Pyramid Creek. I should have put the scepter I found in the bag with these guys and not in my pocket. PHOTO BY AMBER LEE JOHNSON.

Land Type: Mountain forest
County: Pierce
GPS: Site A: N47 6.765' / W121 25.634', 3,819 ft. (druzy); Site B: N47 6.266' / W121 27.882', 3,324 ft.
Best Season: Late spring through fall
Land Manager: USFS—Mt. Baker-Snoqualmie National Forest
Material: Druzy quartz, skeletal quartz, agate, chalcedony, geodes
Tools: Geology pick, heavy hammer
Vehicle: 4WD
Accommodations: Camping in area
Special attractions: Mt. Rainier; Chinook Pass
Finding the site: From WA-410 east of Greenwater take FR-70 northeast for 10.2 miles. At the fork take it to the left onto NF-7060 to get to Site A. The quartz in the talus is 2.2 miles up this very steep road. Site B is reached by taking the fork to

the right and continuing on NF-70 for about 1.4 miles. Take a left onto NF-7065. In 0.3 mile you will see a pullout to your left. Follow the hill about 0.25 mile down to the outcrop and the talus below it.

Rockhounding

This site is very close to the Greenwater collecting area and can make for a nice addition to a multiday trip or just a visit on its own. The view at the top is spectacular and the quartz crystals are very interesting. There is also agate, jasper, and petrified wood in the area. Not a lot of people come back to this site because they get caught up at the many digging opportunities at Greenwater. I think with some more exploring of the area this could turn out to be a great site.

Site A has druzy quartz pockets in the host rock. Most of the crystals are 2 mm or smaller but sparkle like a pike of diamonds. Some of these pockets can be cut out and cabochons made from them. There are also small (¼ to ½ inch) crystals with skeletal growth. I found a nice ½ inch skeletal scepter point right in the middle of the road. It was quite interesting, but being so

The steep talus at Site A of Pyramid Creek.

small I left in in my pocket and it disappeared doing laundry when I got home. Good thing I found a few other small points. My little truck doesn't get stopped often, but the hill leading up to this site proved too much for her. I had to park half way and then hike the rest of the way up. Along the way I found lots of small but colorful tumbler sized pieces of jasper throughout the road.

Site B has agate nodules, seam agate, and geodes coming out of an outcrop about a quarter mile downhill from the parking area. Hike down the hill until you see a large outcrop. There is material still lodged in there, but also float can be found below the outcrop in the talus. Bring heavy hammers and chisels to remove stubborn agate from the host rock. For more information about the area consult the WSMC maps and Tim Fisher's Ore-Rock-On DVD.

51 George Creek Cliffs

A view of the huge slide that happened at the George Creek Cliffs.

Land Type: Mountain forest
County: Pierce
GPS: N47 4.855' / W121 27.639', 4,035 ft.
Best Season: Late spring through fall
Land Manager: USFS—Mt. Baker-Snoqualmie National Forest
Material: Jasper, purple agate
Tools: Heavy hammer, chisel, gad
Vehicle: Any
Accommodations: None on site, but camping nearby
Special attractions: Skookum Falls Viewpoint
Finding the site: Take WA-410 to just southeast of Greenwater. Turn onto FR-70 and drive 5.8 miles. Take a right onto FS-72 and drive 0.7 mile to a fork in the road. Take FR-72 to the left. Drive 3.2 miles to another fork where you will continue to the left. It's another 1.4 miles to another fork in the road. Take NF-72201 to the left and drive 0.9 mile and take NF-72202 to the right. Drive about 1.4 miles until you see a huge slide area and a place to pull off.

Rockhounding

This is an old site written up by Jackson (1992) and has seen a lot of action over the years. The material here is jasper consisting mostly of the green variety, but other colors can be found. Most of the surface material has long been picked up, but the occasional piece can be found lying around. Most material will need to be chiseled out of the host rock, but you can get some large chunks this way. I hear there is better material up at the bottom of the cliffs, but I was especially clumsy the day I visited and barely made it a quarter the way up the huge boulders. Along my stumbling adventure I did see many veins of jasper embedded in huge rocks.

I cannot even fathom what it looked or sounded like when this mountain gave way and a gigantic landslide happened. The boulders here are huge and there are thousands of them. You can't even imagine how massive this slide is until you see it in person. Use caution when traversing the boulders. Some can be loose and wobbly and will trip you up. This might not be the best spot for young kids. The view and enormity of this site make it well worth a visit along. The fact there's jasper there is just the cherry on top.

Some of the purple agate found way on top of the cliffs.

At the eleventh hour it was brought to my attention by Ed Lehman that there is good material at the top of the cliffs. Even better news is you don't have to climb the cliffs. There is a road that goes almost right to the deposit. At this spot there is a purple agate deposit that gets the most attention. At this spot there is a purple agate deposit that gets the most attention. Ed also tells me there is a stunning variety of brecciated jasper in the same place, but people get so caught up on the purple agate that they tend to ignore the other excellent lapidary material. To get to this spot follow the directions to George Creek Cliffs. At the junction of NF-72201 and NF-7226 take NF-7226 to the right and drive about. You then follow a trail on the north side right to the digging area. If you don't have the WSMC maps you should. Contact the Washington State Mineral Council to obtain one. All the proceeds go to keeping the Walker Valley area open to rockhounds.

52 American River

Typical American River chalcedony.

Land Type: Forested river gravels
County: Yakima
GPS: N46 57.817' / W121 16.048', 3,274 ft.
Best Season: Spring through summer
Land Manager: USFS—Okanogan-Wenatchee.
Material: Chalcedony, agate
Tools: Geology pick
Vehicle: Any
Accommodations: Camping throughout area; lodging in Yakima
Special attractions: Mt. Rainier; Chinook Scenic Byway
Finding the site: From Enumclaw, take WA-410 approximately 59.0 miles east towards Yakima. Just before mile marker 83 look for a bridge and park on the southwest side to your right. More gravel can be accessed from Hells Crossing Campground just across the highway.

Rockhounding

The American River, a tributary to the Little Naches River, weaves its way alongside WA-410 for many miles and has numerous agate collecting opportunities. I came upon this spot returning home from a wonderful recon daytrip to the Little Naches River area looking for colorful agates and thundereggs. For the GPS location listed here, I used the easiest and most accessible pullout that I could find. Be on the lookout as there are many other places to pull-over along the byway and explore along the long winding river. Make sure to bring at least one friend to keep a sharp eye out for gravel bars while you drive. I tend to get easily distracted by gravel bars when driving alone and that is just not safe for anyone. It's always helpful to have a copilot watching for those good spots.

This would be an excellent spot for the whole family to hunt at while traveling or on a scenic daytrip from the Ellensburg or Yakima areas. Take some time on your drive and do some exploring to find good places to access the river. Google Earth can be an excellent tool for this site when preplanning

Searching for chalcedony and agates in the American River.

a trip. Please watch the little ones if they go in the river. Although it's fairly shallow, the current can get strong.

The only ever so slight drawback to this site is that the agate here is mostly clear to just slightly yellow toned. Without any patterns or banding in them, this material would be considered clear chalcedony. A few specimens that I found here had a small bit of banding in them making them true agates, but not many. The upside to this site is its ease of river access and seemingly plentiful material to be found. I filled my pockets full of good tumbling material in just about a half hour of collecting and that was only from one gravel bar. I imagine you could fill a large tumbler full of material with a good day of exploring the many abundant gravel bars of the American River. There were many more bars worth exploring, but I started to run out of good agate hunting light and headed back to my folks place after a long day of stimulating exploring.

53 Little Naches

Gotcha! An agate you couldn't miss in the Little Naches River.

Land Type: Forested hillside, river gravels
County: Yakima
GPS: Site A: N46 59.417' / W121 5.867', 2,566 ft. (Little Naches Campground);
Site B: N46 1.643' / W121 9.228', 2,796 ft. (Longmire Meadows Campground); Site
C: N47 1.648' / W121 5.846', 3, 850 ft. (thundereggs)
Best Season: Spring through fall
Land Manager: USFS—Wenatchee National Forest
Material: Thundereggs, agate, chalcedony, jasper
Tools: Pick, shovel, geology pick
Vehicle: Any for river access; most for the thunderegg deposit
Accommodations: Camping throughout area
Special attractions: Salmon Falls Interpretive Site

Rockhounding

I absolutely love the Little Naches River area and very much wish I would have spent some time there when I lived relatively close by in my youth. The area is scenic and beautiful. There's lots of wildlife to observe. I love the curvy and steep drive over Chinook Pass; I always have. Last but certainly not least is the wonderful rockhounding. There is a lot of agate and jasper in the river and as long as you can get to gravel you should do well. There is also a thunderegg deposit just up in the hills. Thundereggs are relatively rare in Washington, at least compared to the amount found in Oregon. Most of the Washington t-egg sites prove to be full of duds, expensive to obtain a permit to access timber land, or just downright impossible to get to. For the thunderegg collector in Washington, this is a must visit site.

The thundereggs here are often called geodes by locals. Although many of them have geoidal centers, they are in fact thundereggs. I hear the opposite in Oregon where I live as locals tend to refer to any geode they see as a thunderegg. The eggs at this site have a nice grey-blue agate centers, sometimes with banding or water-lines. They take a great polish as well. You have

My frog friend checking out the agate I pulled out of the Little Naches River.

A cut baby thunderegg from the hills above the Little Naches River. (Appleyard collection).
PHOTO by LOGON APPLEYARD.

A large and beautiful thunderegg dug from the pits at Little Naches. Photo by Logon Appleyard.

to dig for the thundereggs. Once you find the pits choose a spot and start digging. A good pick comes in handy at this site. You have to break away a lot of the host rock to get to the eggs. Check the WSMC maps for other lesser known egg deposits in the area. Nearby there is a green variety of rhyolite with tiny thundereggs embedded in it. It slabs well and can be cut into cabochons.

The river hunting here is like anywhere else. Find gravel and cover a lot of ground. The best gravels at this area tend to be on the other side of the river. Prepare to get wet if you want to access these bars. The agate and chalcedony found here can be clear, yellow, grey, blue, and any combination of the colors. The agate and chalcedony make for excellent tumbling material. A few thunderegg pieces have been found in the river as well. Whole eggs may exist in the river, but they will be difficult to identify if they have been worn down by the river. Broken bits with exposed agate are much easier to identify. The jasper here is typical of the northwest; multicolored and brecciated, but most commonly found in red tones. Some chunks big enough to cut slabs and cabs from can be found.

54 Timberwolf Mountain

Land Type: Mountain meadow
County: Yakima
GPS: N47 45.211' / W121 8.351', 4,780 ft.
Best Season: Late spring through fall
Land Manager: USFS—Gifford Pinchot National Forest
Material: Quartz crystals
Tools: Geology pick, shovel, trowel, screen
Vehicle: 4WD suggested
Accommodations: Camping throughout area
Special attractions: Mt. Rainier National Park
Finding the site: On US 12 about 12 miles west from the US 12/WA-410 junction, take NF-1530/Bethel Rigde Rd. to the north for about 15 miles staying on the main line the whole time. Nile Rd connects with US 12 at two points, so coming from either direction look for the first turn, but if you miss it there will be another. Take Nile Rd. to NF-1500. It will be just a few miles from either direction on Nile. Drive the main line the whole time on NF-1500 for about 15 miles. Take a right onto NF-190 and drive 1.7 miles to NF-633 on your left and a huge meadow. The quartz is about a ¼ mile walk down to the bottom.

Rockhounding

This is one of the two sites in the book I did not make it to. Two years in a row I kept putting it off till late in the season and each year by the time I was ready to head on up it had started snowing already. The collecting area is at a high altitude and the snow can hit very early. The last planned trip, I called the forest service to ask about snow and the woman who the phone scoffed at me for the notion that I would even have to ask. Plan your adventures to Timberwolf Mountain better than I did. Even though I did not visit the site I know plenty of people who have, they always find something, and I'm confident adding it to the list of rockhounding sites found in this book. I tried getting shots of this site from friends, but they were all to low quality to send to print. This site will be first on my list when I update the book in the future.

The quartz crystals found at Timberwolf Mountain aren't ever very large, but they are very clear and can make for some excellent jewelry points. If you are looking to get larger crystals, clusters, and interesting crystal formations I would suggest going to Hansen Creek or attending one of Bob Jackson's

Geology Adventures to the Spruce Ridge Claim. If you live in Yakima or the surrounding areas, this site would be a lot closer to get to than the sites at Snoqualmie Pass.

There are two methods of attack when it comes to finding crystals here. You can cover as much ground as you can walking and stick to surface scores. A good time for this would be just after a lite rain. It will wash dirt and dust of the quartz and make them sparkle, especially if the sun comes out right after the rain. The second method is to dig and screen dirt. The idea here is to process as much dirt as you can. Two people always make for a more efficient screening process, but then you have to split the crystals at the end. Whichever method works best for you, I'm sure you'll find plenty of clear pretty quartz crystals.

55 Icicle Creek

Land Type: Mountain forest
County: Chelan
GPS: N47 32.632' / W120 47.776', 2,967 ft.
Best Season: Late spring through fall
Land Manager: USFS—Wenatchee National Forest
Material: Black tourmaline, feldspar
Tools: Heavy Hammer, paleo pick
Vehicle: Most
Accommodations: Camping in area, lodging in Leavenworth
Special attractions: Leavenworth
Finding the site: From US 2 just west of Leavensworth take Icicle Creek Rd to the south. Drive 8.4 miles and then take a left onto NF-7600. Continue for 0.1 mile and take the fork to the right on NF-7601. Drive about 1.8 miles until you see a pullout on your left. Backtrack by foot down the road. You will start to see boulders in the field above you.

Rockhounding

There are reports of blue beryl and rose quartz producing pegmatites in the same general area as the tourmaline and feldspar. I drove around the mountain but couldn't find any signs of pegmatites, which is usually the glitter of mica. After searching for what seemed like forever, I gave up on the beryl. I would like to go back to the area and do some more exploring. Maybe it just wasn't my day to find pegmatites.

The tourmaline in feldspar comes in absolutely huge chunks. You can either try to muscle a giant piece off the hillside and back to your vehicle, or you can hammer and chisel out more manageable-sized pieces. I guess it all depends on what you plan on doing with the material. Solid areas in the rock you might be able to cut slabs from. The black and white rock would make for some striking cabochons if it holds together. I suppose carvers could use it. Again the black and white could produce some stunning carvings. Mostly the material is good yard rock. Grab a big piece to put in your garden. You can then stand proud with your chest puffed up, push up your glasses up (if you wear them), point at it and say, "I have Washington tourmaline."

The nearby village of Leavenworth is near and dear to my heart. My grandfather was born in the small Nordic town and my great-aunt Maxine

Sites 55-61

lived there her whole life. We would visit her often when I was a child. My grandfather ended up meeting my grandmother at WWU, they moved to Warm Beach, and eventually, that is where I would pick up rockhounding. Leavenworth is now a Bavarian Alps style tourist village, but it is still wonderful. In the village, the building in which my family ran a creamery still stands to this day. There is now a fancy restaurant on top and a dive bar on the bottom, just how I like it; the best of both worlds. I highly recommend a visit to this quaint little village. There is even a rock shop there now.

56 Douglas Creek

Land Type: High desert
County: Douglas
GPS: N47 27.774' / W119 52.419', 1,123 ft. (parking area and trailhead)
Best Season: Spring through fall. Avoid high temperatures
Land Manager: BLM—Spokane District
Material: Agatized wood, opalized wood, common opal
Tools: Geology pick, shovel, pick
Vehicle: High clearance
Accommodations: Primitive camping throughout BLM land
Special attractions: The Gorge Amphitheater
Finding the site: From US 2 take H Rd SW to the south. This is about 4.4 miles east of the town of Douglas. H Rd will eventually turn into Slack Canyon Rd SW. The parking area at the falls is about 11.4 miles in. For hillside collecting pull over anywhere once you're on BLM land. You used to be able to reach this location from the south through Palisades, but it's a very rough road that is washed out just before you reach the site. Unless you have a beefy ATV and a brass pair, I don't recommend this route.

Rockhounding

The falls at Douglas Creek are a very welcome desert oasis in dry and dusty land that is eastern Washington. The creek has carved its way through the local bedrock creating wondrous shapes and multiple channels shooting off as waterfalls. You can hike way down the creek to find tempting clear plunge pools just screaming to be jumped into. I can confirm that I heeded the watery siren's call a few times. But be fair warned that the southern end of the falls is popular with local and traveling sun enthusiasts; that is, those folks who prefer to spend their time in the sun with no clothes on. That being said, besides some people on ATV's far in the hills, I did not run into anyone during my visits here. I also cannot confirm, nor deny if my clothes stayed on during my visits.

The best material you are looking for is excellent agate replaced petrified wood. The material you will most likely find is opalized wood, that is very nice but can be crumbly and not hold up to lapidary uses or tough travel. The prize agate material is very hard and will take a great polish. Most of the wood

A view of Douglas Creek from the parking area above it.

in this area comes in brown and tan colors and can often be mistaken for real wood. Be sure to inspect anything that looks like buried wood.

There are two modes of collecting in this area. The first is scouring the hillsides above the creek. Just about anywhere along your drive in that may look promising, or you see a lot of rocks scattered around, pull over and do some inspecting. Make sure to hike around and cover some good area. If you start finding wood at the bottom of a hillside, follow it up and see if you can find the source it had weathered out of. This method can be tough in high heats, so plan your trip accordingly.

The other way to find rocks here is to follow the creek. There are lots of big curves and pools where creek tumbled gravel collects. A snorkeling mask may come in handy in some of the larger pool areas where there's abundant

One of the many waterfalls found at Douglas Creek.

Wild jasmine gowning by the creek made a lovely scent in the air.

gravel accumulated. I wouldn't advise hiking down the creek alone, especially if no one else is in the area. Be smart and bring a friend, as it would be tough to get out alone if you get injured. Just about anywhere you can park near the creek that has gravels are worth inspecting. My GPS marks a parking area, which also has a trail that leads way down into the canyon. Also, remember that you may encounter some new friends in the creek with their birthday suits on.

57 Rock 'N' Tomahawk Ranch

Land Type: High Desert
County: Kittitas
GPS: N47 9.654' / W120 38.063', 2,744 ft.
Best Season: Spring through fall
Land Manager: Private
Material: Ellensburg Blue Agate, jasper
Tools: Geology pick, gem scoop
Vehicle: Any
Accommodations: Camping in area
Special attractions: None
Finding the site: From I-90 take exit 106 for US 97 N toward Wenatchee. Take University/US 97 0.7 mile then take a left onto Reecer Creek Rd. Stay on Reecer for about 11.2 miles to the gate of the ranch.

Rockhounding

If you're not familiar with Ellensburg Blue Agate, then put this book down, Google that, then get back to me. It is one of the most coveted agates, or mineral for that matter, in the Pacific Northwest. Every rockhound knows about it and every rockhound wants a piece. The agate is an astonishing cornflower blue and a stone with deep saturation can fetch an even more astonishing price nowadays. The source of the agate has never been discovered and the only place you can find them is the Ellensburg dirt.

Many moons ago the ranchers of the Ellensburg Valley were okay with people coming onto their land to hunt for silly rocks. All was well until some bad apples knocked down fences and left holes that can be very dangerous for livestock. The ranchers understandably closed their land to rockhounds as it began to cost them money. Nowadays, unless you are fortunate enough have family or friends that own land in the Ellensburg Valley, just about the only place you will find accessible agate hunting land is going to be at the Rock 'N' Tomahawk Ranch.

The agate ranch asks that you call ahead and make a plan. They don't do walk-ins. They only charge a modest daily fee per person. Call them at (509) 962-2403 for more information and current pricing. They will provide you with a map of where you can dig on their land and show you some specimens so you will know what to look for. Digging is not allowed, so you must cover a lot of ground in hopes of finding the elusive blue agate. Harsh winters help get the stones to the surface. Rare Ellensburg rains can help with the hunt, as any agate is easier to notice when wet. Plan on doing a lot of walking and don't hold your breath for any excellent agates. It's not valuable because people find it all the time. It's valuable because it's rare and beautiful much like my beloved wife.

Nick Zentner, a Central Washington University geology professor, has a wonderful lecture video about the elusive blue agates and it is a must watch. You can easily find it and many other videos about the geology of the northwest he had made on YouTube. Even better, try to sit in on one of his lectures.

58 First Creek

A whopper of a geode found at First Creek. (O'Brien collection)

Land Type: Mountain forest
County: Kittitas
GPS: N47 12.605' / W 120 40.409', 2,753 ft.
Best Season: Spring through fall
Land Manager: USFS—Wenatchee National Forest
Material: Agate, chalcedony, quartz geodes, calcite, thundereggs
Tools: Geology pick, paleo pick, heavy hammer, chisel
Vehicle: Any
Accommodations: None on site; camping nearby
Special attractions: Historic Liberty
Finding the site: From I-90 west of Cle Elum take exit 85. Turn onto WA-10/WA-970 and follow it for 11.4 miles. Be sure to take WA-970 to the left when it splits off from WA-10. The parking area will be on the left. Park here then walk through the gate. The site is a 1.3 mile hike up this road. Don't cross the creek and stay to your left. You will start to see signs of where people trekked up the hill.

Rockhounding

First Creek is a vast area with lots of hidden treasures and even more land to explore. I only had a half a day to check out this site, so I chose a spot the shortest hike from the road. There are many more deposits in the area and some prospecting may turn up something new. Consult Tim Fisher's DVD for lots of waypoints around First Creek. Ed Lehman showed me some slabs and cabs from a deposit on the south side of the creek. Apparently, there is a slightly known thunderegg spot with low quality "locality" specimens, but the eggs he showed me were from another newer site in the area. Before he pulled them out he said that they could rival any thunderegg from Oregon. I quietly scoffed at the notion. He then pulled them out and my jaw dropped. They really could give Oregon t-eggs a run. Although heavily fractured they had beautiful moss and plumes similar to eggs from both Richardson's Rock Ranch and the Lucky Strike Mine. The slabs they had cut were beautiful and the cabs absolutely stunning. I can't wait to get back to the First Creek area and find the site.

The spot I listed here is known for quartz geodes and some agate nodules. Some of the agate can be botryoidal and if covered in tiny quartz crystals and

A lovely agate nodule found at First Creek. (McFarland collection). PHOTO by DAVID McFARLAND

can be quite mesmerizing. Search the lower part of the hill for float all the way up to outcrops at the top of the hill where you can work fresh material out. Be cautious climbing around the outcrop at the top. There are some very steep parts. I know I was worried about slipping and tumbling at a few points. The hike up the hill can be exhausting especially after walking over a mile just to start going straight up. You're going to need to be in good physical condition for this site if you want to make it up the steep hillside.

Hopefully, someday they will open the gate to this site again and people can really start to do some exploring. There is so much material along this creek already known and who knows what is waiting to be found. For now, we will just have to be content with the short hike in.

59 Crystal Mountain

Land Type: Mountain forest
County: Chelan
GPS: Site A: N47 13.925' / W120 37.578', 4,967 ft. (Crystal Mountain); Site B: N47 15.110' / W120 35.168', 6,347 ft.
Best Season: Late spring through fall
Land Manager: USFS—Wenatchee National Forest
Material: Agate, chalcedony, jasper, quartz, calcite, zeolites
Tools: Geology pick
Vehicle: 4WD recommended
Accommodations: Camping throughout the national forest
Special attractions: Teanaway Community Forest
Finding the site: From I-90 in Ellensburg take exit 106 toward US 97/ W University Way. Take this 0.7 mile to Reecer Creek Rd. Stay on Reecer for 15.2 miles to FR-3500. Take a right onto the forest service road and travel 1.3 miles to a fork in the road. For Crystal Mountain stay to the left on NF-3507 and continue for 4.3 miles until you see a road on your left heading up the hill. You can drive up this as far as you are comfortable, or you can park back on the main road. The collecting area is only a 0.3 mile hike up the hill from NF-3507. To get to Lion Rock you will stay to the right on NF-3500 at the NF-3507 junction. Travel 1.9 miles where you will take a left onto NF-35 / Table Mountain Rd. Drive 3.8 miles and take a left onto NF-125. Head 0.7 mile up to the top.

Rockhounding

This site covers a lot of area and some really cool specimens can be obtained here. The views are beautiful and with such good material, I'm surprised this site isn't hunted more by Washington Rockhounds. There are a lot of other great rockhounding sites in the area and I think this one gets overlooked sometimes. Nearby Lion Rock is over a mile above sea level and is known for having fluorescent calcite. When I visited it was during the day, it was super windy, and I didn't have my UV light packed. I wasn't able to locate much calcite. Be cautious at Lion Rock at night because there are very steep drop-offs all around you there. Falling down on one of those would be bad enough, but at night? No way.

Finding material at Crystal Mountain is very easy. Most people just cover a lot of ground and surface hunt. There is material all over the hillside and it even goes down the other side to the west. There are reports that you can access this area from Liberty Road off of WA-97, but when I checked out the area there were a lot of claim markers (it's gold country) and it just seemed like a super sketchy place to be. I felt like someone was watching me the whole time I drove around trying to find good access and there probably were people watching. I may have just taken a wrong turn, but I just didn't like that lower area.

The agate and chalcedony here is generally clear to gray tones, I have seen some from here that are light blue color with the occasional splotch of red. I have also seen some agates that are almost black. Most of the agates have banding, many are botryoidal, but there are some with the occasional black and /or white plumes inside and make for wonder display specimens or cabochons. The banded stuff does as well. There are many agate geodes with clear quartz crystals lining the inside. Sometimes there can be calcite crystals as a secondary growth in the geode over the quartz. The quartz here can occasionally get somewhat large. I have seen crystals up to an inch or two

The steep road leading up the collecting area at Crystal Mountain. Just park at the bottom and walk up.

from here and many of them with inclusions. The jasper here leans toward the brown and tan tones. I have seen many pieces of jasper from here that remind me of some of the Owyhee Picture Jasper in deep southeastern Oregon. Some of them with blue tones you don't really see in Oregon material. Red jasper is also commonly found here, some with black/gray streaks in it.

Bob Jackson reports Ellensburg Blue Agate in Reecer Creek, which you will be near to on the way in. The big problem is most of it is on private land and the locals don't take too kindly to people agate hunting anymore. Once you get into national forest land, you start heading away from the Creek. There is a spot at a big curve headed up NF-3500 that crosses the creek. The national forest is just a few hundred feet north of here. It may be worth checking out.

60 Red Top

An extremely nice banded blue agate from Red Top Mountain. (Kittleson collection)

Land Type: Mountain forest
County: Kittitas
GPS: N47 18.372' / W120 45.617', 5,224 ft.
Best Season: Spring through early fall
Land Manager: United States Forest Service
Material: Agate, chalcedony, quartz geodes, jasper
Tools: Pick, shovel, geology pick
Vehicle: Any. Northwest forest pass required
Accommodations: None on site; camping in area
Special attractions: Red Top Fire Lookout
Finding the site: Take US 97 to just north of Mineral Springs Campground and the resort. Take NF-9738 to the west and drive 2.6 miles where you will take a slight left onto NF-9702 and continue 3.7 miles to the parking area. Follow the trail for about a mile and you'll be right in the beginning of the digging area.

Rockhounding

Red Top is tops with many northwest rockhounds. I think that Lanny Kittleson of NW Rockhounds is actually in love with the blue agate from here. It has been a popular rockhounding area for many years, for those seeking agates and geodes it still continues to produce beautiful material. The views are wonderful from this spot, so do not forget to bring a camera. The fire lookout here is pretty impressive and you can even volunteer to be on watch, but you would not be able to leave your post and dig for agates. It sure would be a fun place to stay though.

The agates here are pretty awesome. The best ones are the deeply blue colored agates. Many will have a light shade of blue, but the nodules with deep blue saturation are stunning, to say the least. You will find lots of grey, light yellow, and clear agate. The only problem is you won't really know what is inside until you cut them. I mean you can smash them to find out, but why would you do that? Don't be silly. The patterns in Red Top agate come in quite a variety too. I have seen many forms of banding, eyes, botryoidal agate and some sweet parallax or shadow agate. Parallax is an optical phenomenon

The Teanaway Ridge is well known for its lovely blue agates and geodes.

that happens when the bands in the agate form extremely thin and close together and end up creating a movement or "shadow" effect on the surface of the stone. You can really only see this when the rock has been cut and polished. Many of the agates at Red Top are geodes filled with clear quartz. There is also a very nice variety of red jasper mixed with agate, or jasp-agate as we say in the northwest. The jasper can be quite spectacular and will create excellent cabochons.

From the parking area there is a short steep hike to the beds. There is a spot that might give those with height issues the willies, as my mother would say. Over all, it's not too bad of a hike in. Along the trail you will encounter a connecting trail going down a steep hill. I did not check this spot out, but I'm told there is good material down there. You will easily begin to notice the digging area when you start to see evidence of digging. The surface material here, for the most part, has long been picked up. There will be the occasional ground score, but for the better material you are going to have to dig. Pick a fresh spot or continue on where someone else was digging. The nodules

The weather can change at a moment's notice at Red Top. I was getting sunburnt just a few minutes before the storm blew in.

here can get fairly large and there are those who only go big, but there are also some people who will bring a screen to sift out everything including all the little cool guys. Some are small enough to cut on a trim saw and are just adorable. Consult the WSMC Wagonmasters Maps for a more detailed map of the digging sites.

61 Old Blewett Pass

Searching for leaf fossils in the road cut on Old Blewitt Pass.

Land Type: Mountain road cut
County: Chelan
GPS: N47 21.056' / W120 40.120', 3,945 ft.
Best Season: Late spring through fall
Land Manager: USFS—Wenatchee National Forest
Material: Eocene leaf fossils
Tools: Hammer, chisel
Vehicle: Any
Accommodations: Camping in area
Special attractions: Old Blewett Pass
Finding the site: Take WA-10/WA-97 north through the town of Liberty to NF-9715 on the north side of the road. Follow NF-9715 for 3.7 miles where you will take a left onto NF-7320. It will be the middle road at the fork. Follow this for about another 0.4 mile until you see a large road cut on your left and a pullout to your right. The fossils are in the road cut.

Rockhounding

This would make an excellent second stop site to visit while hounding other well-known spots in the area. The site is relatively easy to get to, although the road is very curvy. The sites are both road cuts, so there's no hiking.

The fossils here are of Eocene age and a part of the Swauk Formation that is connected to the Chuckanut Formation farther north near Bellingham and the Huntington Formation near Huntington, Oregon. You're mostly going to find whole and bits of leaves and palm fronds. The host rock here falls apart easily, so hold out for larger whole specimens and make sure to bring something to wrap them in. I made the mistake of putting my specimens in a bag in the back of my truck. I intended on getting some good photographs of them back home, but by the time I got there after my long rockhounding mission, I found that they had been smashed to smithereens. Some paper towels and a shoebox would have saved them from destruction. They also do not like the weather, so one you get them home keep them inside, in a dry place, and out of direct sunlight. Being as I didn't get any good shots of the fossils here please see the chapter on Racehorse Creek. The material from there is very similar.

Collecting fossils here is relatively simple. Get some good chunks of the host rock and start splitting them open. The goal here is to split it right on a fossil bearing zone of the rock. Some people are more fortunate at finding respectable fossils than others. I am a part of the latter. That being said, no one should walk away from this site without at least a couple good fossils. The creeks in the area are also known for having gold in them. Bring your pan and give some of them a shot. Watch for claims in the area.

62 Umtanum Creek

What most of the petrified wood looks like that you will find at Umtanum Creek.

Land Type: High desert
County: Yakima
GPS: N46 51.350' / W120 28.925', 1,382
Best Season: Spring and fall
Land Manager: BLM—Spokane
Material: Petrified Wood
Tools: Geology pick, paleo pick
Vehicle: Any. Discovery pass required
Accommodations: Camping in area
Special attractions: Umtanum Creek Recreational Area
Finding the site: This site is reached via WA-821 from Ellensburg, 13 miles to the north or Selah, 16 miles to the south. Make your way to the Umtanum Creek Recreational Area. Pull into the site and find a parking spot near the footbridge at the end of the lot. Cross the bridge, and from here you can follow the trail in the middle running alongside the creek. You can take the Umtanum Ridge Trail to the left, or you can scamper up the path to the right.

Rockhounding

Umtanum Creek and Umtanum Ridge above it have long been known by local rock clubs for the excellent petrified wood that comes out of those very steep hills. There are other spots the local clubs like to go to, but you're going to have to hook up with them to find out where they are. This area should keep you plenty busy with a lot of area to cover.

The petrified wood from this area is excellent. It is hard and will take a great polish. The cellular replacement is superb and material still looks very woody. It can range for tumbler size bits to full rounds several inches in diameter. I have now been to this site three times. Each time seems hotter than the last and I have only walked away with a handful of tumbler material. That being said, I have a fried who came here once, barely even went up the hill and found a full round 3 inch across and about a foot long. I wanted to slap him when he sent me a picture text message.

Your best bet for a successful hunt is to cover a lot of ground. These hills are more for mountain goat types. Some spots were steep enough I would slip

Cross the bridge over the Yakima River and head to either side of the creek in search of Umtanum Creek petrified wood.

Sites 62-66

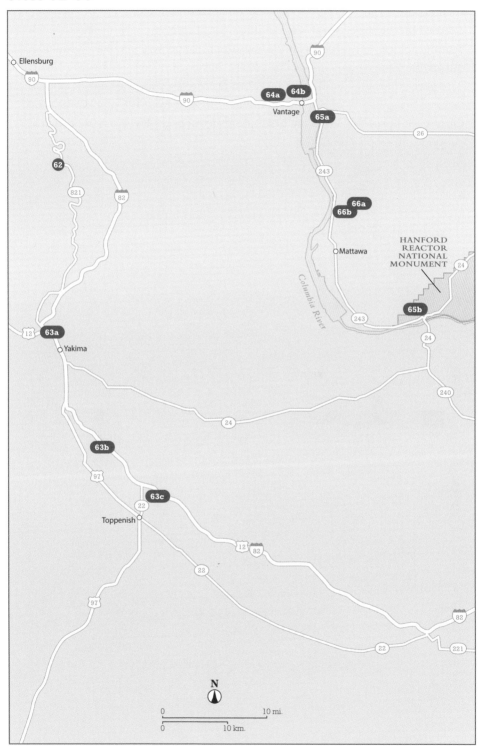

Ellensburg

90

64a 64b

Vantage

65a

26

62

821

82

243

66a
66b

HANFORD
REACTOR
NATIONAL
MONUMENT

Mattawa

24

Columbia River

243

65b

12 63a

24

Yakima

240

24

63b

97

63c

22

Toppenish

12
82

22

82

97

22
221

N

0		10 mi.
0		10 km.

back down the hill sometimes. Wander the steep hillsides looking for anything exposed on the surface. You can run into a lot of icebergs here, so inspect everything poking out. That small log my friend found was just barely sticking out of the ground and he says he almost missed it. Keep your eyes peeled. This gets extremely hot in the summer, so try to plan your trips during cooler seasons. Bring plenty of water and sunblock. Take it from Ol' Uncle Lars; because I got burnt to a crisp my first outing at this site. Maybe it wasn't such a good idea to stop there in July.

63 Yakima River

A banded agate found in the Yakima River.

Land Type: River gravel

County: Yakima

GPS: Site A: N46 37.497' / W120 30.078', 1,060 ft. (Rotary Lake Park and Ride) Site B: N46 28.01' / W120 23.981', 849 ft. (Donald), Site C: N46 24.109' / W120 17.074', 749 ft. (Zillah)

Best Season: Summer or low water levels

Land Manager: Washington State—Department of Natural Resources

Material: Agate, jasper

Tools: Geology pick

Vehicle: Any. Have a discover pass with you just in case

Accommodations: Lodging in Yakima

Special attractions: The Yakima Nation

Finding the site: Site A: From I-82 in Yakima take exit 31A. Turn south onto N 1st St and drive 0.1 mile. Take a left onto E R St; drive 0.8 mile and take a left onto E

Frwy Lake Rd. Drive about 0.3 mile to the park and ride. You can park here further up on the Yakima Greenway. Work your way to the river and see if you can find a place you feel comfortable crossing. It all sort of depends on the height of the river at the time. Site B is reached via I-82 from exit 44. Turn south onto Donald Wapato Rd. and drive 0.3 mile to a parking area on the northwest side of the bridge. Follow the trail below the road to the river. Site C: From I-84 take exit 52. Head south on N Meyers Rd for about 0.1 mile. There will be a parking area on the northwest side of the bridge.

Rockhounding

The sites listed here provide easy access to the Yakama River and her bountiful gravels. One can find a fair amount of good tumbler material here. The big drawback I found about these sites was the hike from the parking area to the river at Sites B was super nasty. There was a ton of garbage and at moments I felt like I was walking through a toilet. I really had to watch my step. Once to the water, it wasn't so bad. Keep your head up when walking gravels close to bridges. I saw on more than one occasion a bottle fly out of a car and smash against the rocks below. As I write this I don't feel like I'm selling this site very well at all. With the drawbacks, the Yakima River itself is a lovely river and if you can get away from the bridges and garbage it's not half bad. A kayak would be a good way to get to some otherwise inaccessible gravel bars and away from the hustle and bustle.

Material here consists of agate, chalcedony, jasper, and petrified wood. The agate and chalcedony here are generally in the tones of clear, yellow, or grey. It is reported that the very rare piece of Ellensburg Blue Agate can be found here, but don't hold your breath. The jasper is typically in the red, brown, and tan tones, but other colors may pop up as well. The petrified wood is excellent and takes a great polish. Most of what you will find here will be of tumbler size, but large chunks are found now and then. Some of the larger jaspers can make wonderful cabochons.

Check out various pullouts along the Yakima River for more access to gravel. Google Earth comes in hand for this. While a kayak or raft can get you to some awesome gravel bars, most of the southern side of the river belongs to the Yakima nation and unless you are a tribe member, I wouldn't recommend

The gravel of the Yakima River can get coated white making searching difficult.

rockhounding on the Nation side of the river. If you are a tribal member there are some excellent rockhounding opportunities in the reservation. The petrified wood I have seen from this area looks so much like pre-petrified wood that I would have been hesitant to reach down for a piece if I saw one in the field.

64 Ginkgo Petrified Forest State Park

A sliced section of petrified wood from the Vantage area that looks like Durante. The museum has quite a collection of pictures found in the local petrified wood.

Land Type: High desert
County: Kittitas
GPS: Site A (museum): N46 57.271' / W119 59.291', 748 ft.; Site B (trails): N46 56.888' / W120 02.199', 1,082 ft.
Best Season: Late spring through summer
Land Manager: Washington State Parks and Recreation Commission
Material: Petrified wood (no collecting)
Tools: None
Vehicle: Any
Accommodations: Camping and RV hookups in Vantage
Special attractions: Gorge Amphitheater

Finding the site: Coming from Seattle or Spokane take I-90 to exit 136 to Vantage. Turn onto Main St/Vantage Hwy and drive 0.7 mile to Ginkgo Road. Take a right and it is about 0.2 mile to the museum. To get to the hiking area continue down Vantage Hwy another 2 miles and you will see the parking area to your right.

Rockhounding

There's good news and bad news about this site. Bad news first; you can't collect here. The good news is it is super awesome place to visit, there are cool petrified logs to see, there's a museum, and it is pretty close to Saddle Mountain where you actually can collect petrified wood. Word has it that across the river at the Iron Horse wayside you can find small pieces of petrified wood in the hills, but digging a hole up there would be greatly frowned upon.

The massive deposits of huge petrified trees along the Columbia River near Vantage were first noticed by highway workers in the late 1920s. The great Civilian Conservation Corps were called in, excavated petrified wood and built a museum. The park was opened to the public in 1938. A "desert rat" by the name of Frank Walter Bobo knew the petrified wood in the well

The Gingko Petrified Forest State Park. Notice the wood they used to the foundation of this sign.

and was commissioned to collect, cut, and polish specimens for the museum. He got to keep half of what he prepared and years later his son inherited a collection of over a ton of petrified wood.

The Wanapum Dam on the Columbia River reached completion in 1963 and of course, the water levels of the river rose. The rising river threatened to submerge petroglyphs that were once above the water line. Around sixty petroglyphs were saved and many of them ended up at a then newly built interpretive center at the site. In October of 1965, the National Park Service declared the Ginkgo Petrified Forest a National Natural Landmark. Ten years later state legislature named petrified wood as the Washington State Gem.

The park museum currently has many cut and polished specimens of the local petrified wood, many of which look like silhouettes of famous people. The salvaged petroglyphs can still be seen at the museum. Near the museum is Ginkgo Gem Shop where you can see large local specimens of petrified wood and purchase small samples of the local material and other minerals from around the world. Further up the road the park continues with two available hikes. The short hike is a 1.5-mile loop and the long hike is a 2.5-mile loop.

Petroglyphs that were saved from the rising river can now be seen at the Gingko Museum.

Along this well-paved hike one will be able see exposed sections of prehistoric Lake Vantage featuring twenty-two species of petrified wood logs left right where they were found in the 1930s.

When I visited this site for the book my mother and her partner Dennis joined us for a walk down the petrified forest trail. At the beginning of the trail there is a sign that warns of rattlesnakes being present in the area. I took notice of the sign, but I knew we were in a snake country already and didn't think much of it as I rarely see snakes on my travels. On our walk out we came upon the sign again and what do you know there's a rattlesnake right underneath it! Yes, a rattlesnake directly under the very sign warning about it. It was also warning us of its presence with a loud rattle. We kept our distance, got around it, and got the heck out of there.

65 Columbia River—Sand Hollow

Searching the gravels of the mighty Columbia River for agates, jasper, and petrified wood.

Land Type: Riverbed gravels
County: Grant
GPS: Site A: N46 55.612' / W119 57.320', 576 ft. (Sand Hollow); Site B: N46 38.366' / W119 44.734', 412 ft. (Vernetia Boat Launch)
Best Season: Any
Land Manager: Grant County Public Utility District
Material: Agate, jasper, petrified wood, granite, quartzite
Tools: Geology pick
Vehicle: Any
Accommodations: Camping on site and in Vantage
Special attractions: Gingko Petrified Forest State Park; The Gorge Amphitheater
Finding the site: From I-90 across the bridge from Vantage take exit 137 for WA-26 E. Drive about a mile and then turn right onto WA-243 S. Go 0.3 mile and the recreation area will be on your right.

Rockhounding

This site is kind of funny for me. First off I discovered this spot totally by accident. My wife and I were on our way to the Tri-Cities area from Wenatchee and I needed to use a bathroom. Just south of the Vantage Bridge was what at first just looked like a simple rest stop. I pulled in, used the facilities, and then quickly realized there was gravel not easily seen from the highway. After hounding for a short while it hit me. This is the spot we used to swim and party at back in the day when we would go to concerts at the Gorge Amphitheater. I have a lot of foggy memories from this place. I even had a flashback of my friend, John Dukes, finding a small piece of petrified wood in the river when we were like sixteen attending a Rat Dog show. The Grant County Public Utility District has now spruced the old party spot up and I must say I like it a lot. It's now paved, has bathrooms, camping is allowed now, there are picnic tables for day use, and best of all access to wonderful Columbia River gravel.

Upon reaching the gravel we quickly found good material. Keep your eyes peeled for agate, chalcedony, jasper, petrified wood, granite, quartzite, and

A well-rounded agate found in the sand near the Columbia River.

A small cache of material collected in the Columbia River near Vantage.

We were just about to leave when I found this cool guy. The rest of our hunt on the Columbia River just got better from then on.

much more. I only listed what my wife and I found in about a half hour and there could be potential for more. The gravels of the Columbia can be from just about anywhere. Whether it eroded out of the rivers many miles of river-bank or it was carried in by ancient floods there is a huge variety of rock to choose from. Take plenty of time to wander the gravel deposit in any direction. Bring some good water shoes or rubber boots for wading in the river for access to more gravel.

This site would be a great place to camp while attending shows at the amphitheater or to just quickly visit while traveling through the area. Just across the bridge is the Gingko Petrified Forest State Park and well worth a visit.

66 Saddle Mountain

A small, yet lovely piece of Saddle Mountain petrified wood.

Land Type: High desert hills
County: Grant
GPS: Site A: N46 47.902' / W119 52.867', 1,991 ft. (NWRH Pit); Site B: N46 47.699' / W119 53.726', 1,991 ft.
Best Season: Late spring through fall
Land Manager: BLM—Spokane
Material: Petrified wood
Tools: Geology pick, shovel, paleo pick, chisels
Vehicle: High-clearance 4WD recommended
Accommodations: Camping in area; lodging in Vantage
Special attractions: The George Amphitheater
Finding the site: From I-90 take WA-243 south from the other side of the bridge from Vantage. Drive about 15 miles into Mattawa and take a left (east) onto Rd. 24 SW. Drive 2 miles then take a left onto R SW. At about 3.0 miles in you will see the BLM sign. From here it's 1.8 miles to the turn for Site A and 1.9 miles for the

turn to site B. For Site A head up the very steep hill for 0.3 mile to a tower. Here take the road to the very left and drive about 0.3 mile and the pits will be on the right. For Site B take the turn to the left at the fork. This will continues you on Rd. R SW. Go for 0.2 mile to an intersection. Take the road on the left, drive approximately 0.5 mile to a spur to the right. Take this right to the diggings. If you see a fat man in a wheelchair; you've gone too far.

Rockhounding

The Saddle Mountains have long been known for their abundance of excellent petrified wood. Just about anywhere on this mountain you will find some sort of ancient fossilized tree. You can try your luck wandering the hillsides to surface material. Check any suspect pieces as mineral icebergs can be common here. That little piece showing might be massive under the surface. The other method of attack here is to dig. You can prospect for a suitable dig spot of your own or you can continue on holes that people were digging before. Either way, you're going to have to move a lot of dirt. The goal is to pull out a perfect full-round log, but a big broken chunk can be quite beautiful as well. Heck, the small pieces are nice too. Do some exploring down the many roads on the mountain. There is private land in the area so please respect posted areas.

The fossil wood here is agatized, hard, and takes a great polish. From bookends, to display pieces, to cabochons; this wood can do it all. The cellular replacement is excellent and some specimens can look just like actual wood. It comes in tones of brown, tan, yellow, cream, and white. Broken chunks are common and can be anywhere from tumbler size to giant logs. Full rounds are not common, but you can score some giant chunks that broke away from big logs.

The two sites I listed here just get you to a couple parts of the mountain worth exploring. Site B is an old well-known spot that still produced excellent material. Site A I call the NW Rockhounds Pit only because we dug here during our 1st Annual Meet Up. Someone else discovered it long ago; I'm just giving it a name. There are many spots on this mountain to did, and possibly many more yet to be found. Do some exploring and keep your eyes peeled for signs of digging, washes, and trails that shoot off into seeming nowhere. For more detailed maps of the area please consult the WSMC maps and the Ore-Rock-On DVD.

A view from the top of the Saddle Mountains.

This is the site that the NW Rockhounds group had their first annual meetup. It was here that I met for the first time some of the people that I will know, dig with, and do business with for the rest of my life. Little did I know then that in the near future I would end up planning the group's annual meetups and become an administrator of our absolutely huge Facebook group. I am very grateful for this group of magnificent people and look forward to many years of rockhounding with them. If you are not familiar with this group please find us on Facebook or visit the NW Rockhounds headquarters, shop, and lapidary school in Seattle.

67 Golden Horn Batholith

A big chunk of rock with a chrysocolla coating. I walked right past this. Glad I have my wife.

Land Type: Alpine mountains
County: Okanogan
GPS: Site A: N48 30.858' / W120 38.564', 5, 181 ft. (big curve parking); Site B: 48 31.351' / 120.64577', 4,916 ft. (Milepost 164)
Best Season: Summer through early fall
Land Manager: USFS—Okanogan-Wenatchee National Forest
Material: Aegirine, apatite, astrophyllite, calcite, chrysocolla, epidote, fluorite, galena, hematite, magnetite, malachite, molybdenite, okanoganite, opal, pyrite, quartz, smoky quartz, siderite, wulfenite, zektzerite, and many more
Tools: Heavy hammer; chisel; gad, pry bar, geology pick
Vehicle: Any
Accommodations: Camping nearby; none on site
Special attractions: Diablo Lake
Finding the site: From east or west take WA-20 to just past/before milepost 163 there will be a huge curve bellow Liberty Bell Mountain with parking on the outside of the curve. Site B is just 0.7 mile downhill from Site A near milepost 164.

Rockhounding

I must start by pointing out this was the absolute most brutal hike I've ever done while researching rockhounding spots in the northwest. The particular hill we climbed was extremely tough hiking up, but was an absolute nightmare hiking back down. If you are familiar with my book *Rockhounding Oregon* you may have read about how I got stuck in the high desert in remote southeastern Oregon and had to hike 10 plus miles to safety with no water and no food. Well, this was much worse. We were pretty beat up after this particular adventure.

That being said, I really want to keep going back. My wife and our Papillion are both absolutely over it, but the gigantic list of minerals that can be found from this area, especially the smoky quartz crystals, keeps me intrigued and wanting to endure even more of the high altitude alpine punishment. There are some seventy-two valid minerals listed on mindat.org that have been found in this collecting area. I listed the more known ones in the material section of this site, but I highly recommend checking them all out

A view of Liberty Bell from the parking area at Site A of the Golden Horn Batholith. We hiked up to the bottom of the cliff face.

My wife, Amber, thinks we should have gone the other way. I should listen to her more often.

Sites 67-69

A view of Kangaroo Ridge from across the valley on the Liberty Bell talus.

on the internet. On our trip we found epidote, aegirine, massive quartz, tiny clear and smoky quartz crystals, chrysocolla, malachite, and azurite. Only a small percentage of what can be obtained at this site.

Site A parking is at a big curve in the road just below Liberty Bell Peak. You have a couple options here. You can go way up the mountain like I did. Unless you're the mountain goat type, I really don't recommend this route. As I mentioned it's pretty brutal. The other route is to head through the forest in the valley. Explore any talus you may encounter for signs of mineralization. Have a good hammer with you to break open the hard granite to expose crystal bearing areas. I have also been told that about halfway up Kangaroo Ridge there is good material and in the cirque east of Cuthroat ridge. Have fun going up to both of those spots. Just about anywhere out here has potential.

Site B extends from milepost 164 to almost 168. Find anywhere to safely pull off the road and find your way downhill wherever you find large boulders. Bust them open and see what's inside.

68 Methow River

Jasper, conglomerate, quartzite, and granite found in the Methow River.

Land Type: High desert river

County: Okanogan

GPS: Site A: N48 32.618' / W120 19.411', 1,963 ft. (upper Methow); Site B: N48 20.890' / W120 6.426', 1,561 ft. (lower Methow)

Best Season: Late spring through fall

Land Manager: Washington State—Department of Natural Resources

Material: Granite, jasper, agate, conglomerate, porphyry basalt, quartzite

Tools: Gem scoop, geology pick

Vehicle: Any

Accommodations: Camping and lodging in area

Special attractions: Winthrop, the cutest town in the world

Finding the site: I think most people will be coming to this area from the west over Washington Pass on WA-20. Site A is a small pullout on the NW side of a bridge that crosses the river by Goats Creek Rd. This is about 5.0 miles west of the turn for Mazama. Headed west it would be 8.2 miles from the intersection in

Winthrop, the cutest town in the world. To reach Site B, take WA-20 to Twisp. At the outside of the curve going through town take Twisp Carlton Rd. and drive 1.3 miles to a public fishing area on your left just before the curve. Park here and walk to the gravel.

Rockhounding

The Methow River winds its way for 80 miles from the north Cascades to Pateros where it dumps out into the mighty Columbia River. I listed two sites to get you started. If you like what you're finding you can follow the river south along WA-153. There are a lot of gravel bars along this river and a lot of places the road crosses. Watch for good pullouts near gravel deposits. But as it always seems to be, the gravel bar is on the other side. It's good to have a cool buddy with you that can spy for gravel while you drive. Or maybe you can be that cool guy.

At Site A the river gravel is much larger than further downstream. We found porphyry basalt and multicolored conglomerates the size of watermelons. We didn't see much in the way of silicate material here, but the rocks we explored

A view of the Methow River at Site B.

here were huge and smaller agates and jaspers can get lost in the mix. I'm sure some cool minerals can be found by smashing open rocks with signs of mineralization or amygdules. There are a lot of interesting things in the mountains where this river is born. At Site B the material gets much smaller and very well river worn. There is a mix of seemingly everything. We found a lot of dark-red brecciated jasper, granite, quartzite, conglomerates, and signs of quartz and agate. There is also a lot of what looks like picture jasper but is not picture jasper, well it's not jasper, but it is picturesque. There is the possibility of some rose quartz working its way out of the Chiwuch River and its tributaries.

I had read some vague reports of garnet in Texas Creek just off of WA-153. We checked the area out, but found it was very difficult to find access to the creek that wasn't on private land. Out of the two spots we could get to, one was iffy if it was private property or not and the other was very grown over and a real bushwhack to get to. We didn't have a pan with us so we tried sampling some of the gravel with our bare hands. We found very quickly that the water was ice cold. After many frozen fistfuls of sand, we didn't see any sign of garnet. Maybe it was the wrong Texas Creek. Maybe we just needed to have a trowel and a gold pan. I'm not sure, but it's worth some more investigation.

69 Chewuch River

A small handful of goodies found in Chewuch River. The rose quartz (bottom center) gets lost in my pink cold hands.

Land Type: Forested river
County: Okanogan
GPS: N48 40.387' / W120 8.182', 2,237 ft.
Best Season: Late spring through fall
Land Manager: DNR, DFW, USFS
Material: Granite, unakite, quartz, rose quartz
Tools: Geology pick, gem scoop
Vehicle: Any
Accommodations: Camping throughout area
Special attractions: Winthrop, the cutest town in the world
Finding the site: From WA-20 at the intersection in the middle of downtown Winthrop continue forward onto Bridge St. and drive 0.2 mile. Take a right onto Bluff St. that will turn into Eastside Chewuch Rd. and stay on it for 6.2 miles. Take a left to stay onto Eastside Chewuch and drive 0.2 mile. Take a right onto NF-51 and

drive for 8 miles. You will see Chewuch Campground on your right. Pull in and find the day-use area if it is busy, or park out by the entrance on NF-51.

Rockhounding

The Chewuch River gets its name from the Columbia-Moses word *cwáx*, which means "creek." Yes, it's named Creek River. I was hoping it was fed by Stream Creek, but that didn't happen.

I came upon this site while trying to reach Junior Creek and Twenty-Mile Creek. I had read a very small mention of good rose quartz coming out of the aforementioned creeks. I got to this area late in the season (late October) and the snow had already hit. The road leading in wasn't too bad, sans the large trucks making their way out. When I found the road leading up Junior Creek, it looked horrible and I was not in the mood to get stuck. I moved my way up the road to find the same road conditions leading up to Twenty-Mile Creek. At first I was a bit disappointed. While I had more sites down the road that was a long drive to get blocked by snow. I then thought to myself, the rose quartz must be working its way into the river. We found a better road on the

Search the gravel of the Chewuch River for lovely pink rose quartz.

west side of the river and drove until we found a decent spot to check at the Chewuch Campground.

At first all we found was granite and white quartzite. There is a lot of "salt and pepper" granite found all over Washington and this site was no exception. It was everywhere. The upside is the granite here was very bright and colorful. I would think some large pieces would make for some excellent carvings. We weren't at the site long before I was about to give up. The water was freezing and with higher water levels there wasn't a whole lot of exposed gravel. Then, as usual, my wife found what we were looking for. It was small, about a half inch, but sug nubbitz it was undoubtedly rose quartz and quite gemmy at that. She also managed to find a small, but very clear quartz. Rumor has it there are quartz crystals in the area. As for me, I found lots of granite, quartzite, and a couple pieces of unakite. When the weather is nice, I highly suggest finding a good gravel bar on Junior or Twenty-Mile Creek. I know I will be in the near future.

I have to end this by mentioning that my wife and I both agree that the nearby town of Winthrop has got to be the cutest town that ever existed. It is set up to be touristy, but we don't care. The quaint old-timey western motif they have going on works for us. We would highly suggest staying in Winthrop while rockhounding the Creek River. I can see our family visiting this town a lot in the future.

70 Frosty Creek

Quartz crystals are common at Frosty Freek, but hold out for nice specimens.

Land Type: Steep rock outcrop
County: Okanogan
GPS: N48 33.107' / W118 59.428', 3,108 ft.
Best Season: Late spring through fall
Land Manager: Washington State—Department of Natural Resources
Material: Quartz, agate, chalcedony, calcite
Tools: Heavy hammer, chisel, geology pick
Vehicle: 4WD suggested
Accommodations: None on site; camping in area
Special attractions: Republic
Finding the site: Take US 97 to Tonasket. Turn onto WA-20/6th St. East and drive 13 miles to Aeneas Valley Rd. Take Aeneas for another 13 miles. Turn left onto Frosty Creek Rd. and travel 1.0 mile and take a right. Drive 1.3 miles up the hill until you see a large outcrop on the top.

Rockhounding

This is not really a site I would go far out of my way to get to, but if you are in the area traveling or possibly visiting friends and /or family then this spot makes for a good place to get some rockhounding done. If anything the view from the dig site is spectacular. I actually spent quite a bit of my time at this site just standing on one the large outcrops and staring off into the distance with wonderment. Do not forget your camera if you should decide to visit this site. Be cautious of any children or dogs you may have traveling with you. There are some very steep parts up there and I once even almost went tumbling down the hill. Okay, maybe twice.

There is a lot of quartz and agate here, but nothing is of extreme size or quality. We found a sparkly clear quartz cluster with crystals about ¼ inch, but most of what we found was light druzy quartz. The agate and chalcedony can be found in a nice light blue color. I managed to find a few pieces large enough for tumbling. My wife found a large geode half that had a big calcite crystal in it. We found out when we got home that the calcite glows yellow under UV light.

A beautiful way to end the day at Frosty Creek. Photo by Amber Lee Johnson.

Sites 70-74

I'm not sure if my wife is trying to keep her balance, doing a dance, or both at Frosty Creek.

When you arrive at the collecting site decide which way you want to walk. Material can be found both above and below the road. There is a bit of float material still on the surface, but I'm guessing all the big stuff was picked up years ago. With some due diligence and spread out searching, one may be able to score something nice on the surface. You can also try busting material out of the outcrop or in larger talus boulders. Search around until you see signs of mineralization in the host rock and then try to knock it out with some heavy hammers and chisels. The quaint old-timey western motif they have going on works for us. We would highly suggest staying in Winthrop while rockhounding the Creek River. I can see our family visiting this town a lot in the future.

71 Stonerose Interpretive Center

A slab of multiple fossils found at the Stonerose dig site. Slabs with so many fossils in one are not easy to come by.

Land Type: Road cut
County: Ferry
GPS: N48 38.869' / W118 44.374', 2,548 ft.
Best Season: May 3–21; May 24–Labor Day; September 7–October 29; 8 a.m.–5 p.m.
Land Manager: Friends of Stonerose Fossils
Material: Eocene fossils
Tools: Chisel, hammer
Vehicle: Any
Accommodations: Lodging in Republic; camping in area
Special attractions: Sherman Pass Scenic Byway
Finding the site: Take either WA-20 or WA-21 to Republic. The interpretive center is on the NW corner of the highway and N Kean St.

Rockhounding

A road in the quaint little town of Republic cuts right through an Eocene fossil bed. The locals set up a 501c3 nonprofit organization called the Friends of Stonerose Fossils and an interpretive center, in order to protect this non-renewable resource. There is a modest fee to dig and kids under 5 are free. Children 18 and under, seniors, and college students with valid college ID receive a discount. Educational groups can call for special rates. You must sign in before 3 p.m. to dig. The dig site closes at 4 p.m. and the center closes at 5 p.m.

After you sign in and pay at the interpretive center, they will give you directions to the fossil deposit just up the hill. You can rent tools from them or bring your own. The best tools are a hammer and a cold-chisel, but people also use paint scrapers, flat head screwdrivers, and many other things to wedge the shale apart. Once at the site you need to start splitting shale. The center will show you the best way in which to do this. There are covered picnic tables at the site for shade, working material, or having lunch.

Stonerose is a great place for the whole family to visit, learn about the local fossils, and dig some of your own.

The fossil digging area just up the hill from the Stonerose Interpretive Center. You must check in and pay at the center before digging.

When done with your dig you must bring all your specimens back to the interpretive center for analysis. They want to make sure they know what is coming out of the dig site and want to let you know what you found. In the end, you get to keep your favorite three specimens and the rest are donated to the center. Should you happen to discover a new species, the center will keep the fossil, but you will be credited for finding it and maybe even possibly have it named after you if you're lucky.

The Stonerose Interpretive Center also has a museum featuring their local county. The town was once a bustling gold town and was a rare one to keep going on after the rush. They even have a good number of minerals such as quartz, amethyst, and fluorite that were found in the area. I didn't have time to check out any of the sites the minerals were from, but with a little research and the right maps, one could have quite the prospecting adventure.

72 Columbia River–Kettle Falls

Stinky Dedos seem to like all the various colors of aventurine we found in the Columbia River near Kettle Falls.

Land Type: River gravel

County: Stevens

GPS: Site A: N48 35.571' / W118 7.436', 1,289 ft.; Site B: N48 34.221' / W118 6.812', 1,214 ft.

Best Season: Late spring through fall

Land Manager: BLM—National Parks Service

Material: Aventurine, quartzite, jasper, agate, chalcedony, epidote, unakite, concretions

Tools: Gem scoop, geology pick

Vehicle: Any

Accommodations: Camping on site; lodging in Kettle Falls

Special attractions: Grand Coulee Dam

Finding the site: From US 395 in Kettle Falls take Boise Rd./Boise Cascade Rd. South. This is the road on the east side of the bridge and river. Drive for 1.9 miles.

Take a left onto Kettle Park Rd. and drive 0.4 mile. Take a right onto Delaware Ave. and drive 0.2 mile, turn right, another 0.2 mile, turn left and it will be 0.3 mile to the parking area.

Rockhounding

The Old Kettle Falls National Recreation Area is not only picturesque, but there's some decent rockhounding as well. Be sure to stop in at the ranger station along Boise Road and let them know you're in the area rockhounding. Not only can they suggest some good spots, but they also have a display of the local unusual concretions.

This northern stretch of the Columbia River supplies the rockhound with something not often found further downstream: aventurine. It is found mainly in tones of green, but brown and purple can be found as well. While not near the quality of most imported aventurine found in rock shops, the green material is slightly translucent when cut into slabs, and could make for some interesting cabochons. The purple material had a nice color to it and would also make some interesting cabs, but it was not translucent as the green.

My wife filling her sack full of rocks at the Columbia River.

A small slab of green aventurine from the Columbia River.

I have yet to cut any of the brown. The aventurine found here tends to be very smooth and when in the water looks a lot like very fine jade. As usual, we found lots of granite and quartzite. The granite was mostly "salt and pepper," but the quartzite came in a variety of tones. We found very little agate or jasper, but it is there. We visited late in the season and with this being a popular camping area I'm sure that the easily seen agates were long picked up.

There is excellent camping in the area and a boat launch. I often wish I had a boat to get to those hard to reach gravel bars. Maybe you should try. Maybe you should bring me with you. While there visiting the park check out the Locust Grove group site. There you will find the remnants of where Kettle Falls used to be located before the Grand Coulee Dam was built. After the damn was installed the area flooded and the town had to move uphill. It is one of the few river towns to survive after the damn was built in the 1930s.

73 Winchester Creek

Blue beryl in matrix found on the ground at Winchester Creek.

Land Type: Forest road cut
County: Pend-Oreille
GPS: N48 21.029' / W117 30.220', 4,774 ft.
Best Season: Late spring though summer
Land Manager: USFS—Colville National Forest
Material: Mica, schorl, albite, smoky quartz, blue beryl
Tools: Geology pick; small hand rake
Vehicle: High clearance
Accommodations: Sporadic campsites along road
Special attractions: Colville National Forest
Finding the site: From WA-20 at the intersection for the turn to Usk, go the other way (west) onto Beeman Rd./McKenzie Rd. Follow this road for 7.1 miles. Turn right onto Flowery Trail Rd. and drive about 3.7 miles to a fork. Take it to the right to continue on Co Hwy. 9517. Go another 6.3 miles where you will see glittery mica and a big hole in the road cut.

Rockhounding

I had been reading about his area and its minerals for many years, but never made it up to that part of Washington to rockhound until I had to for this book. This area in remote northwest Washington provides a rare occasion in the state to find blue beryl crystals. Gem quality blue beryl is known as aquamarine, but the crystals here are mostly very cloudy to almost opaque. I did find one crystal that could have some very small zones in it that could be called aquamarine, but overall the crystal is cloudy beryl. Now that I've got you all excited for blue beryl, here's the downside. You can't really dig at this site. It's in a road cut and the forest service in these parts doesn't very much appreciate people digging into the road cut and especially knocking loose material into the road. They have been known to issue tickets. Not messing this site up will ensure it doesn't get closed down in the future. Please do not go here and dig more into the pegmatite no matter how tempting it is. I was tempted too, but I managed to find some awesome minerals just looking in the tailings and around the road. This is just one spot out of many you may find in the area. Do some exploring down the winding mountain roads and keep an eye peeled for glittering mica.

By far the most common mineral you are going to find here will be mica. It is everywhere and is one of the best indicators of pegmatites where cool minerals live. The mica is going to get all over you and your clothes. If you collect some and leave it in your hoodie pocket for a while, everything you touch with become glittery. I looked like I had just attended Oregon Country Fair after I was done with this site. Try to find large books of mica for

My collection of loose blue beryl found near the road cut at Winchester Creek.

anything worth bringing home. I found a few up to a couple inches wide and about a quarter inch thick. There is going to be a lot of white albite feldspar at this location. I didn't find any crystals of the albite, but it may be possible. There is also a fair amount of smoky quartz found here, but it is not particularly gemmy and was just small chunks mixed with feldspar. I did manage to get enough sizable pieces of smoky quartz that I believe with tumble nicely. Schorl, or black tourmaline, crystals will be found throughout the pegmatite mix, but don't get your hopes up for intact crystals. The material is very brittle and mixed in with the feldspar.

The real prize here is blue beryl. Hexagonal crystals are the most highly prized, but most will be broken bits of crystals. I was not very much expecting to find any of the elusive blue stone at this site, but sag nabbit I did. I actually found my first two pieces in matrix very quickly just examining some of the rubble someone should not have been digging out of the road cut and let roll down the hill. I arrived at this site late in the day and the sun was setting in just the right way. My wife and I always like to call it "agate hour," but it seemed to work with the blue beryl as well. I spent a fair amount of time just leaning into the hill and letting the sun do the work. I managed to score three crystals of blue beryl this way, in fact, one was the largest of the trip.

The road cut pegmatite found at Winchester Creek.

Since digging at this site wasn't really an option and being as I got there late in the day I decided to grab some of the bigger chunks of pegmatite that were lying around in the road and tumbled down from where people have dug before. My wife and I smashed some of it into smaller chunks and wouldn't you believe it, we found some blue beryl crystals in matrix. We often enjoy bringing rocks home to play with on days we can't get out rockhounding.

74 Pend-Oreille River

A very nice piece of purple quartzite found in the Pend-Oreille River.

Land Type: River bank
County: Pend-Oreille
GPS: N48 18.945' / W117 16.666', 2,035 ft.
Best Season: Spring through fall
Land Manager: Usk General Store
Material: Quartzite, jasper, granite
Tools: Gem scoop
Vehicle: Any
Accommodations: Camping in area
Special attractions: Colville National Forest
Finding the site: Off WA-20 just north of the junction with WA-211 and south of Cusick take 5th St./Kings Lake Rd. about 0.6 mile. Just before the bridge you will see the general store. Stop here first and pay the park fee.

Rockhounding

This site makes for a great family spot to stop, swim, float, fish, have a picnic, and pick up a few tumbled river rocks. It is also close to the Winchester Creek site and would be a nice secondary stop. I probably wouldn't travel a long distance for just this site. The view is very nice and the river is easy to wade in to look for stones. There is a modest fee to park at the site, but I think it's worth it. The fee can be paid at the Usk General Store right above the site.

I must admit I'm not much of a quartzite kind of guy. I usually find it pretty uninteresting, but some people like it. This site may have changed my mind a bit. The quartzite here seemed a bit more colorful than I was used to and the stones were nice and smooth. Then just as I was about to leave I found the most purple piece of quartzite I've ever found. It may not seem like much, but it was pretty enough to make even me look for quartzite. I managed to wrangle up a couple more purple pieces and was more than happy with my treasures. The more common colors of quartzites here have nice warm yellow, orange, and red tones. I also found a bit of brick red jasper and some granite.

There are many more access points on the Pend-Oreille River if you really want to do some exploring or maybe just have a more private spot to do your thing.

The bridge leading to the reservation from the collecting area near Usk.

APPENDIX A: GLOSSARY

Agate: A type of microcrystalline quartz exhibiting a pattern or inclusions such as banding, moss, plumes, and so forth. Clear "agates" are technically chalcedony.

Azurite: A deep blue copper carbonate hydroxide, formed in the oxidized portions of copper deposits.

Banded Agate: Agates with multiple layers of alternating colors.

Basalt: The most common igneous rock on Earth's surface.

Botyroidal: A mineral habit exhibiting a globular external form resembling a *bunch of grapes* as derived from the Greek.

Brecciated: To form into breccia; a type of rock made of broken fragments of minerals or rock cemented together by a fine-grained matrix.

Calcite: A type of calcium carbonate.

Carnelian: A red to orange translucent variety of chalcedony, which is usually colored by iron oxides.

Chalcedony: A type of microcrystalline quartz without banding or inclusions. Clear chalcedony nodules found on Oregon shores are commonly referred to as "beach agates."

Chalcopyrite: A copper iron sulfide generally brassy in color.

Concretion: A round mineral mass formed in sedimentary rock. Concretions often contain marine fossils that they form around.

Dendrites: A tree-like habit mineral inclusion usually formed by manganese or iron oxides.

Epidote: A calcium aluminum iron silicate hydroxide generally found in a light to dark green color.

Feldspar: A group of aluminosilicate minerals. The most common mineral found in the Earth's crust.

Float: Refers to mineral collected on the surface of the ground.

Fortification Banding: A type of banded agate with sharp angular corners, much resembling a fort.

Fossil: Any evidence of past life preserved in rock, including bones, shells, footprints, excrement, and borings.

Garnet: An abundant silicate mineral found in metamorphic rock.

Geode: A hollow cavity within rock that is lined with crystals.

Granite: The most common intrusive rock in Earth's crust. The three main minerals it is made up of are of feldspar, quartz, and mica.

Iceberg: Term used by rockhounds for a specimen that on the surface only reveals a portion of its true size.

Inclusions: A crystal, mineral, or fragment of another substance enclosed in crystals or rock.

Jasper: A variety of opaque microcrystalline quartz.

Matrix: The rock or sediment in which a mineral, gemstone, or fossil is embedded.

Micromount: A term used by mineral collectors to describe mineral specimens that are best appreciated using an optical aid, such as a hand lens.

Moss Agate: A variety of agate with moss-like inclusions, usually formed by chlorite or manganese oxides.

Opal: A type of hydrated amorphous silica.

Outcrop: Part of a geologic structure that shows itself on the surface of the Earth.

Petrified Wood: Ancient wood that has had its cells completely replaced by silica turning it into agate, jasper or opal.

Pit: A hole that rockhounds dig in.

Plume Agate: A variety of agate with feathery plume-like inclusions usually formed by chlorite or manganese oxides.

Pyrite: A brassy colored iron-sulfide. Also known as "fool's gold."

Quartz: A mineral made out of silicon dioxide with a hexagonal crystal structure.

Vug: An open cavity in a rock that will often contain crystals.

Wash: An eroded area of soil caused by occasional running water.

Zeolite: A large family of hydrous calcium, aluminum or sodium silicate minerals. It is usually formed as alteration products of igneous rocks.

APPENDIX B: CLUBS

Clubs are a great way to meet other rockhounding enthusiasts. Many offer classes in lapidary and host field trips all over the state. Some even have their own claims that only club members can dig at. I highly suggest you join one today. All clubs listed were accurate at the time of publication. Please refer to the Northwest Federation of Mineralogical Societies website for up to date information on most clubs.

Northwest Federation of Mineralogical Societies
www.amfed.org/nfms/ClubsOR.asp

Washington State Mineral Council
https://mineralcouncil.wordpress.com

Aberdeen
Grays Harbor Geology & Gem Society
P.O. Box 2003
Aberdeen, WA 98520
facebook.com/GraysHarborGeologyandGem

Bellingham
Mount Baker Rock & Gem Club
P.O. Box 30324
Bellingham, WA 98228
mtbakerrockclub.org

Bellevue
Bellevue Rock Club
P.O. Box 1851
Bellevue, WA 98009
bellevuerockclub.org

Federal Way
Federal Way Gem & Mineral Society
4303 254th St.
Kent, WA 98032

Kent
Cascade Mineralogical Society
14431 SE 254th St.
Kent. WA. 98042
cascademineralogicalsociety.org

Sequim
Callam County Gem & Mineral Association
P.O. Box 98
Sequim, WA 98382
sequimrocks.org

Redmond
East King Co. Rock Club
P.O. Box 2203
Redmond, WA 98073
eastkingco.org

Everett
Everett Rock & Gem Club
P.O. Box 1615
Everett, WA 980206
everettrockclub.com

Kennewick
Lakeside Gem & Mineral Club
P.O. Box 6652
Kennewick, WA 98336

Lakeside Junior Rock Club
P.O. Box 6652
Kennewick, WA 98336
lakesidegemandmineralclub.com

Lynnwood
Maplewood Rock & Gem Club
P.O. Box 5657
Lynnwood, WA 98046
www.maplewoodrockclub.com

Walla Walla
Marcus Whitman Gem & Mineral Society
P.O. Box 338
Walla Walla, WA 9836

Marysville
Marysville Rock & Gem Club, Inc.
P.O. Box 1721
Marysville, WA 98270

Mt. Vernon
North Puget Sound Faceting Guild
P.O. Box 2841
Mt. Vernon, WA 98273
facetguild.com

Skagit Rock & Gem Club
P.O. Box 224
Mt. Vernon, WA 98273
skagitrockandgem.com

Colville
Panorama Gem & Mineral Club
701-B Williams Lake Rd.
Colville, WA 99114
panoramagem.com

Port Townsend
Port Townsend Rock Club
P.O. Box 1383
Port Townsend, WA 98368

Puyallup
Puyallup Valley Gem & Mineral Club
P.O. Box 134
Puyallup, WA 98371

Spokane
Rock Rollers Club, Inc.
P.O. Box 14766
Spokane, WA 99214
www.rockrollers.org/WP

Ellensburg
Rock Wolves
P.O. Box 103
Ellensburg, WA 98926

Seattle
NW Rockhounds
2720 115th St.
Seattle, WA 98125
(206) 364-1440
facebook.com/groups/NWRockhounds

Rocky Trails Junior Rockhounding Club
606 NW 79th St.
Seattle, WA 98117

Seattle Faceting Club
P.O. Box 362
Seattle, WA 98062

North Seattle Lapidary and Mineral Club
P.O. Box 16145
Longview, WA 98116
northseattlerockclub.org

West Seattle Rock Club, Inc.
P.O. Box 16145
Longview, WA 98116
westseattlerockclub.org

Longview
Southern Washington Mineralogical Society
P.O. Box 704
Longview, WA 98632

Olympia
Washington Agate & Mineral Society
P.O. Box 2553
Olympia, WA 98507
wamsolympia.wordpress.com

Whidbey Island
Whidbey Island Gem Club
P.O. Box 224
Oak Harbor, WA 98277

Whidbey Pebble Pushers
P.O. Box 4440 – Honeymoon
Greenbank, WA 98253

Yakima
Yakima Rock & Mineral Club, Inc.
P.O. Box 326
Yakima, WA 98907
yakimarockclub.com

APPENDIX C: MUSEUMS

Dear Washington,
Please put more rocks in your museums.
Forever yours,
Lars W. Johnson

Seriously though there are not enough museums featuring the wonderful minerals found in the great state Washington. Maybe it's time to change that. The following museums should absolutely be visited.

Ellensburg
Kittitas County Historical Museum
114 East 3rd Ave.
Ellensburg, WA 98926
(509) 925-3778
kchm.org

Seattle
Burke Museum of Natural History
17 Ave Northeast & Northwest 45th St.
Seattle, WA 98105
(206) 543-5590
burkemuseum.org

Vantage
Gingko Petrified Forest State Park
4511 Huntzinger Rd.
Vantage, WA 98950
(509) 856-2700
parks.state.wa.us/288/Gingko-Petrified-Forest

APPENDIX D: ROCK SHOPS

Support your local rock shop! Rock shops are not only great places to buy your favorite gems, minerals, and lapidary equipment locally, but quite often the employees can share some local rockhounding information or even provide you with some maps.

Bellingham
Body Mined And Soul
1240 E Maple St. #101
Bellingham, WA 98225 (360) 389-3618

Edmonds
The Wishing Stone
317 Main St.
Edmonds, WA 98020 (425) 712-1060
http://www.thewishingstone.com/

Ellensburg
Ellensburg Agate & Bead Shop
201 S Main St.
Ellensburg, WA 98926 (509) 925-4998

Kent
Jerry's Rock & Gem
804 West Valley Hwy. Kent, WA 98032
(253) 859-1287
www.jerrysrockandgem.com

Moore Than Rocks
315 W Meeker St. Kent, WA 98032
(253) 852-7625
www.moorethanrocks.com

Kirkland
Earthlight Gems & Minerals
46 Lakeshore Plaza Dr. Kirkland, WA (425) 828-3872
www.earthlightgems.com

Langley
Whidbey Island Gems
206 First Street
Langely, WA 98260 (360) 221-0393
www.whidbeygems.com

Leavenworth
Mainz Haus of Rock & Etc.
220 9th St. # D
Leavenworth, WA 98826 (509) 548-1078

Mount Vernon
SkagitLapidary Supply
314 Myrtle St.
Mount Vernon, WA 98273
360-336-3533

Poulsbo
Imagine That
18954 Front St. NE
Poulsbo, WA 98370
360-336-3533

Seattle
Agate Designs
120 1st Ave S Seattle, WA (206) 621-3063
www.agatedesigns.com

NW Rockhounds
2720 NE 115th St. Seattle, WA (206) 364-1440
www.nwrockhounds.com

Shelton
Cove Crystals & Gifts
510 SE Old Arcadia Rd.
Shelton, WA 98584 (360) 426-8111
www.covecrystals.com

Spokane
Irv's Jewelry, Rocks, & Gifts
11907 E Trent Ave.
Spokane Valley, WA 99206 (509) 924-5464
www.irvsshop.com

Munchie's Rockpile Custom Jewelry
604 W Garland Ave.
Spokane, WA 99205 (509) 328-7311

Wonders of the World
621 W Mallon Ave. #412
Spokane, WA 99201 (509) 328-6890
www.wondersoftheworldinc.com

Sequim
Eclipse Minerals
645 W. Washington St. #6
Sequim, WA 98382
(360) 797-1176

R&T Crystals 'n' Beads
158 E Bell St.
Sequim, WA 98382
(360) 681-5087

Vancouver
Celestial Awakenings
6610 NE Hwy. 99
Vancouver, WA 98665
(360) 896-2207
www.celestial-awakenings-crystals.com

Handley Rock & Jewelry Supply
6160 Hwy. 99
Vancouver, WA 98665
(360) 693-1034
https://www.facebook.com/Handleys-Rock-Jewelry-163231580382303

Vantage
Ginko Gem Shop
Ginkgo Ave. Vantage, WA 98950 (509) 856-2225

SUGGESTED READING

Cannon, Bart, *Minerals of Washington*, Cordilleran Press, Mercer Island, WA, 1975

Daniels, Frank J., and Dayvault, Richard D., *Ancient Forests: A Closer Look at Fossil Wood*, Western Colorado, Grand Junction, CO, 2006

Drake, H.C., *Northwest Gem Trails,* Mineralogist, Portland, OR, 1950

Fisher, Tim, *Ore Rock On DVD*, version 5.2, 2011

Gladwell, Jon, *A Family Field Collecting Guide for Northwest Oregon and Southwest, Washington*, Vols I, II, III, Myrddin Emrys, Portland, OR, 2012

Jackson, Bob, *The Rockhound's Guide to Washington*, Vol. 4, Jackson Mt. Press, Renton, WA, 1992

Lehman, Edward, *Wagon Master Maps: All Collecting Sites in Washington,* Washington State Mineral Council, Color Version, 2016

Livingston, Jr., and Vaughn E, *Fossils in Washington*, *Information Circular No. 33*, Washington Division of Mines and Geology, Olympia, WA, 1959

Myers, K.T., and Petrovic, Richard L., *Agates of the Oregon Coast,* FACETS, Newport, OR, 2008

Pattie, Bob, *Gems and Minerals of Washington*, Washington State Mineral Council, Olympia, WA, 1983

Ream, Lanny, *Gems and Minerals of Washington,* 3rd edn, Jackson Mt. Press, Renton, WA, 1994

Romaine, Garret, *Gem Trails of Washington*, 2nd edn, Gem Guide Books, Baldwin Park, CA, 2014

Romaine, Garret, *Gold Panning the Pacific Northwest*, Rowman & Littlefield, Guilford, CT, 2015

Tucker, David S, *Geology Underfoot in Western Washington,* Mountain Press, Missoula, MT, 2015

ABOUT THE AUTHOR

Born and raised in Washington, Lars W. Johnson's passion for absorbing geologic beauty developed early when the family took a trip south to Portland, Oregon, just in time to catch Mount St. Helens erupt in 1980. Decades, and countless rockhounding trips, later, Lars opened a retail rock shop and organized many fieldtrips, inspiring enthusiasm and inclusivity to those new to rockhounding and a renewed curiosity for locating, collecting, and sharing experiences that seasoned rockhounds could appreciate. A blog quickly spawned to share his accumulated rockhounding information and exploring, writing, mapping, and cataloguing became his focus. He is a long-time member and administrator or NW Rockhounds and also belongs to the Mount Hood Rock Club. Lars currently lives in Portland, OR with his wife Amber.

Lars W. Johnson